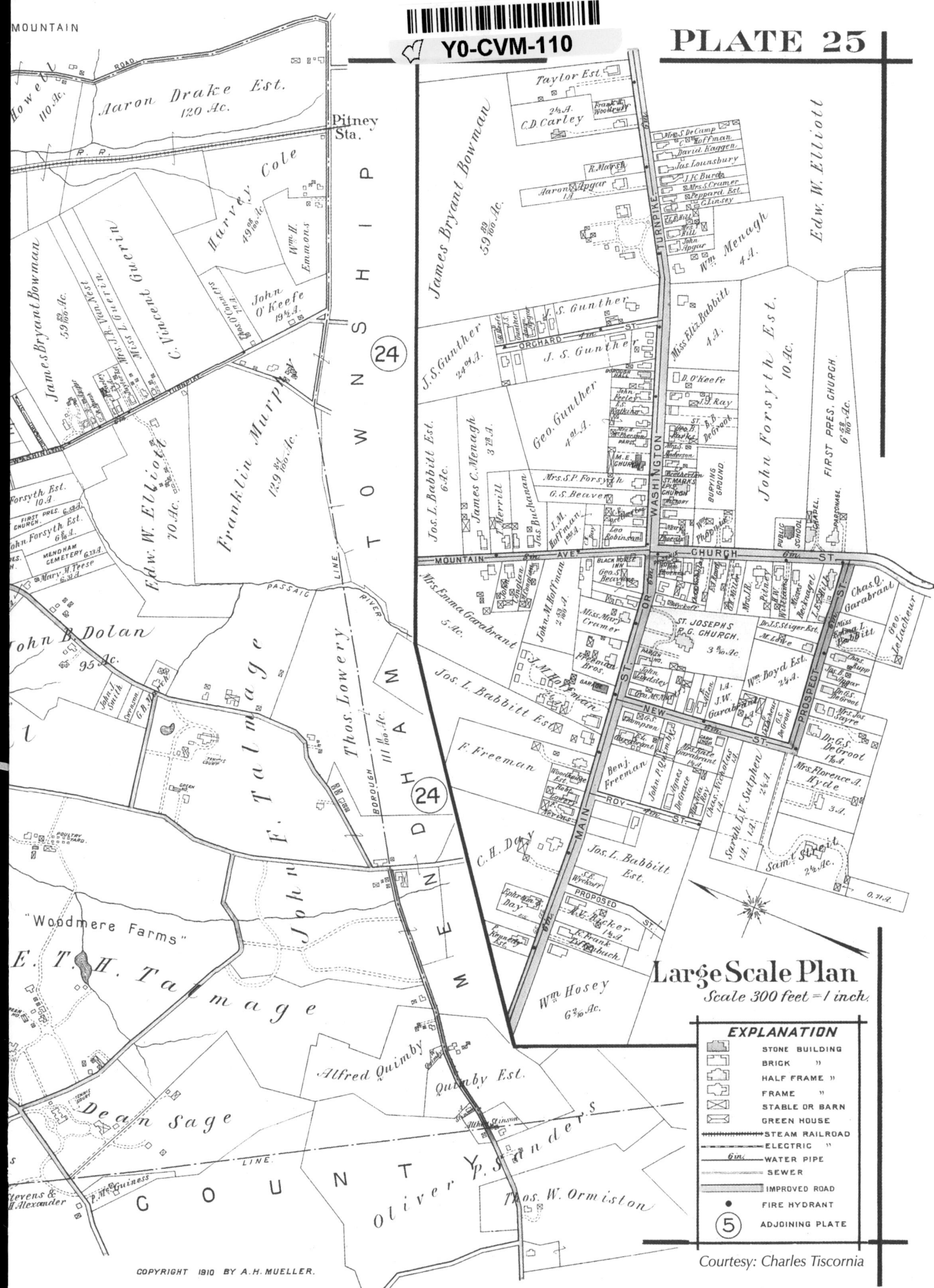

Reflections on a Community

Mendham Borough ◦◦◦ The Centennial
1906–2006

The Borough of Mendham is proud to sponsor this pictorial history, which tells the vibrant story of our special community from early times to modern day.

Reflections on a Community

Mendham Borough ∞ The Centennial 1906–2006

The Centennial Book Committee

John M. Andrus, Chairman
Michael A. Ackerman
Diana S. Callahan
Michael Gaffney
Martin Gertler
Art Gillen
Barbara Nelson
Peggy Oswald
Marie L. Pfeifer
Charles E. Topping

Dedicated

to understanding the past, celebrating the present, and continuing the spirit.

Copyright © 2007 by Borough of Mendham

All rights reserved, including the right to reproduce this work in any form whatsoever without permission in writing from the publishers, except for brief passages in connection with a review. For information, write:

The Donning Company Publishers
184 Business Park Drive, Suite 206
Virginia Beach, VA 23462–6533

Steve Mull, General Manager
Barbara Buchanan, Office Manager
Kathleen Sheridan, Senior Editor
Amy Thomann, Graphic Designer
Mellanie Denny, Imaging Artist
Scott Rule, Director of Marketing
Stephanie Linneman, Marketing Coordinator
Susan Adams, Project Research Coordinator

Mary Taylor, Project Director

Library of Congress Cataloging-in-Publication Data

Reflections on a community : Mendham Borough--the centennial, 1906-2006 / Centennial Book Committee.
   p. cm.
 Includes bibliographical references.
 ISBN-13: 978-1-57864-395-0
 ISBN-10: 1-57864-395-3
 1. Mendham (N.J.)--History. 2. Mendham (N.J.)--Centennial celebrations, etc. 3. Mendham (N.J.)--Social life and customs. 4. Community life--New Jersey--Mendham. I. Centennial Book Committee (Mendham, N.J.) II. Title: Mendham Borough--the centennial, 1906-2006.
 F144.M45R44 2006
 974.9'74--dc22
                           2006030972

Printed in the United States of America by Walsworth Publishing Company

Contents

Reflections on a Community

6   Foreword

8   Mayor's Message

9   Acknowledgments

12   **Chapter One:** Roots of a Village

22   **Chapter Two:** When Grass Grew on Main Street

46   **Chapter Three:** A Walk through Our Neighborhoods

78   **Chapter Four:** Educating Our Children

90   **Chapter Five:** Labor Day

108   **Chapter Six:** The Centennial Celebration

120   **Chapter Seven:** Protecting and Serving

146   **Chapter Eight:** Outdoor Diversions

166   **Chapter Nine:** Community through Common Interests

184   **Chapter Ten:** By the People, of the People, for the People

192   Bibliography

Foreword

The Borough of Mendham, New Jersey, is a community where time seems to have passed more slowly than in other parts of the state. It is a community where the names of the founding families have become the names of many of our streets, where homes sold are often referred to by the last name of the seller rather than by the street address, and where many children return to raise the next generation. It is also the community we call "home"—a description that dates back to the founding of Mendham Borough for many of our resident families.

Whether you are a multigeneration Mendhamite or a family beginning your own traditions in the Borough, each of us can appreciate the special character of Mendham. A community to which people are attracted because of its location, character, and way of life, it is also a place in which residents recognize the need for involvement and where volunteerism flourishes. It is a community that continually invests in itself, supporting local business, recreation, and education . . . celebrating accomplishments and sharing in memories. It is a community that has evolved with the times but has never lost sight of its heritage.

At the center of Mendham Borough stand the landmarks of this community. The Phoenix House, the Black Horse Inn, Robinson's Drug Shop, and the Phoenix Sanford Building . . . all dating back to the beginning of the nineteenth century or earlier. Even more important, they stand as icons of Mendham Borough . . . historic, warm, and welcoming. Perhaps those words are the best ones to describe this community as well.

As we reflected upon the history of Mendham in creating this book, we gained a certain sense of contentment in recalling the facts (and the folklore) of our community. How did Florie Farm get its name? How did the "mud hole" become the mudhole? How many times has the Hilltop Church been hit by lightning? How did each of the neighborhoods develop, and who was responsible for those developments? If nothing else, reflecting upon the community of Mendham puts the character of this community into perspective, helps each of us understand why we are so protective of what we have created together, and why this community will maintain its distinctiveness for generations to come.

Yes, things have changed. Several farms became residential neighborhoods, Gunther Motors became the Audi dealership, Foodtown became Kings, the shopping center replaced the traditional general store, and cars replaced carriages as the primary transportation on Main Street. Yet, despite the changes, the character and camaraderie of Mendham have not changed very much at all. This is still a tightly knit community where neighbors know neighbors, where classes of students often stay together from kindergarten through high school, and where a trip to Kings can take hours as we meet friends in every aisle. It is still a community where the annual Labor Day parade has more marchers than spectators, where residents know the accomplishments of the high school sports teams whether they have children in the school or not, and where so many organizations need meeting space that the Garabrant Center has a committee reservation almost every night.

In this book, you'll read about the founders of Mendham, the families whose names grace the streets, the neighborhoods past and present, and the unique characteristics that make Mendham a special place to live. You'll get a glimpse into the history of this community, and into the way it looked then and the way it looks today. But looks aside, the one thing that remains a constant in Mendham is the feeling of this community.

While so much of the world around us has changed, Mendham has somehow managed to retain the feel of a village— historic but progressive, established but evolving, private yet welcoming. Few other communities seem to have done as good a job of adapting to the times while ensuring that the values upon which the community is based remain intact. Few other places could be as special as this place for every generation.

We have enjoyed our own personal reflection in creating this commemorative book. We hope that you find an equal level of enjoyment as you revisit this book time and again.

—Martin Gertler

Mayor's Message

May 15, 2006, marked the one hundredth anniversary of Mendham Borough, and this book commemorates that event.

Mendham Borough was formed out of Mendham Township one hundred years ago when forward-thinking residents realized the need for a water system not only to serve the community but especially to provide fire protection. Much of the work to form Mendham Borough was begun and performed by volunteer firemen. The tradition of volunteerism continues today with the Borough served by an all-volunteer fire department and first aid squad.

Mendham is blessed with talented, generous people who, for more than one hundred years, have volunteered their time and talents to enrich our community life. Mendham Borough has a unique sense of community, where neighbors know neighbors and residents rally to assist others. That sense of community carries into many committees and organizations that exist only because of residents who care about their town and work hard to maintain it.

A visitor to Mendham Borough coming from Morristown follows a lazy stretch of old Route 24 through rolling hills, forests, and meadows dotted with new and historic homes, estates, and parks. Suddenly, there is a traffic light, and you are entering the village of Mendham Borough. Mendham is a crossroads town that hasn't changed much since the nineteenth century. The crossroads four corners have their original structures, lending a quaint charm to the historic shopping area. This area is today preserved as a Historic District with many homes and buildings listed on the National Register of Historic places.

It is the hope of the One Hundredth Anniversary Team, which put this book together, that it will bring to you a sense of this wonderful town that we all call home.

—Mayor Richard Kraft

Acknowledgments

A year and a half ago, Lem Andrus, a lifetime Essex Fells, New Jersey, resident, brought me a copy of his town's centennial book. As a former resident, I found it was enjoyable to rummage through a volume that recalled long-forgotten events, places, and friends, and it seemed appropriate to make an effort to compile a similar celebration for Mendham Borough's centennial. I'm not certain whether to thank Dad or not. Nonetheless, with the encouragement of Essex Fells chairperson Sharon Ellis, and with the support and funding of the Mendham Borough Council, the project commenced.

Having spent the time to delve into what makes Mendham, Mendham, it became quickly apparent that this book could be, and is, nothing more than a representative sample of the history, organizations, and individuals that have kept the Borough the home that it is. Our purpose is to present longtime residents with some memories and to entice newcomers to explore more vigorously.

If there are any acknowledgments, they must first go to the people and organizations that are not mentioned in the pages that follow. Space, time, and information, as well as the nature of the project, did not allow us to be all-inclusive, but for those involved, it became apparent how many contributors there have been over the years and how impossible it is to recognize them all. We know you are there, and as fellow residents, we offer our gratitude.

Thanks to the committee members who worked tirelessly and consistently to provide whatever was asked of them. Each with a special set of skills and knowledge, they all exhibited the one characteristic that echoed throughout the research for the book—they cared for the town, its people, and its history. Special thanks to Mike Ackerman, Diana Callahan, Mike Gaffney, Marty Gertler, Art Gillen, Barbara Nelson, Peggy Oswald, Marie Pfeifer, and Charles Topping.

None of our research is original, and without prior works, the job would have been virtually impossible. If your interest is in architecture, Jack Turpin and Barry Thompson's two-volume set on the Somerset Hills properties is outstanding in its scope and presentation of the area's country homes. Janet Foster's study of Mendham architecture and John Rae's *Images of America* series book on the Mendhams offer hundreds of historical photographs.

Nearer to home is Ella Mockridge's "Our Mendham" and Mendham Township's "The Mendhams," and no one has chronicled the Borough's history more closely than Kate Emmons in *Through the Years in Mendham Borough*. Her knowledge and collection of information is extraordinary, and for an understanding of local government, it is particularly interesting. The Borough fire department's one hundredth anniversary volume provides a complete chronicle of a most important and vital organization, and various articles and papers by groups such as the Mendham Borough Historical Society and individuals such as Judy Swiencki (Pastime Lanes history) are worth seeking out.

Conversations with town residents were invaluable in obtaining a feel of what Mendham of old was all about. The real history of Mendham resides with the Cillos, Crotsleys, Pennimpedes, Enrights, Smiths, Boltons, Swatsworths, Fagans, et al. In a variety of venues, they shared their memories, and we cannot thank them enough for their cooperation.

With apologies to those inadvertently omitted, a number of key individuals offered a treasure trove of visual images. Don and Newly Preziosi offered freely of their collection of historical Mendham postcards, as did Nick Cusano with his. Rare older photos were received from Ernie Maw and Honey Belton. In addition, Sharon Hakakian, Sam

Vacchiano, the Tufariellos, Bob Marino, Liz Smith, Jenny Gemberling, Barbara Nutt, Kevin Kenny, Jack Kuhn, the Sisters of Christian Charity, Marie Griffin, John Enright, Chris Creamer, Fred Corona, Di Di Sharkey, the Lauermans, Pete Cillo, Joe Szoke, Vi Lioudis, Ginnie Beutnagel, Eileen Lupo, and the Mulcahys. Thanks to all and to the help and contributions from Pat Serrano, Lauren Houdlich, and Chris McManus. The fire department, with the cooperation of Rich DeNicola, Darren Fitzpatrick, and Craig Bellamy, allowed the use of their archives; the police lent their scrapbook; and Dave Crotsley contributed DPW photos. Don Quimby offered family photos, and thanks to Earl Barnes, Ruth Smith, John Smith, Charlie Tiscornia, Carolyn Menagh, Robert Snedaker Jr., and Leo Baehler for their contributions. Bob Cleary has laboriously collected and documented the Pastime Club history; much of that section and Labor Day come from Bob. Special thanks to committee member and photographer Mike Gaffney for spending a number of Saturdays to help out with photographs.

The best history is written by those who lived it, and contributions by Jim Cillo, Doris Mills, Michael Ackerman, and Jeff Andrus, I feel, give an authentic feel for their experiences in Mendham.

It must be noted that this project may not have been completed without the Herculean effort put forth by Diana Callahan. As writer, photographer, interviewer, and Phoenix House contact person, she became the linchpin of the operation. There is no way to express the depth of gratitude.

And finally to Penny—not just for her invaluable knowledge of our residents, not for her ability to get the best from each interview, not for her rapierlike wit in helping decide which photos to include or exclude, but also for her tolerance in allowing this project to disrupt her home—thank you.

—John Andrus

Chapter One
Roots of a Village

Nowhere in all the world is there a lovelier pastoral land than our countryside with its rolling hills, fertile valleys, many streams and a prodigal lushness of native growth. A spot for man to build a home, develop his roots and be a person.

—Ella Mockridge, "Our Mendham"

To limit relating the history of Mendham Borough beginning with its incorporation on May 15, 1905, would be much like a sportswriter reporting on a World Series game from the seventh-inning stretch to the last out. That might be acceptable if the first six innings were scoreless. For Mendham Borough, the beginning of its story predates the incorporation and starts with the history of the Mendhams.

The First Inhabitants

The history of Mendham begins with the Lenni Lenape, who were the first to call Mendham their home. The Lenape were family oriented, community minded, proponents of education for the children, and respectful of the elderly and infirm—not unlike the Mendham we know today. The first native people came from Asia through Siberia across the Bering Strait land bridge down through Alaska, into Washington State and across North America to the East Coast, settling in New Jersey and Mendham.

The first people thrived. Mendham abounded in the essentials for supporting life: food, clothing, and shelter. With soil rich in minerals, the herb and

Somewhere in Mendham, somewhere in time…the youth of Mendham have long been its most important asset. *Courtesy of Ernie Maw.*

Top: Byram Township officials issue an invitation to Mayor Mulcahy (right) to help celebrate Byram Township's 175th Anniversary, 1973. *Courtesy of Terry Mulcahy*

Bottom: Aerial view, Hilltop Church and environs, ca. 1933. *Mendham Borough archives*

vegetable gardens flourished. Even then, Mendham was a special place with the headwaters of two rivers, (the Raritan and Passaic), many ponds, and an abundance of wildlife—small animals, deer, and wild turkeys. From the thick forests, trees were bent to frame the wigwams faced with tree bark. A sixty-foot communal "longhouse" was home for two or three families; men built the houses, and women cared for them and their children.

As children were encouraged to explore nature, Lenape boys hunted with their fathers as early as the age of six. They made their own weapons and canoes. As a coming-of-age rite for boys in this area that would be called "Mendham," they were sent alone into the woods to have a vision and seek a guardian spirit (the spirit of an animal).

The Dutch and the English came. The Lenape had no gold, but they had wealth in fox and beaver pelts to barter for wool blankets, metal tools, utensils, pots and pans, mirrors, glass colored beads, and silver bells. The Indians

The modern-day apple orchard on the corner of Prospect and New Streets. It was one of the first sources to supply area distilleries. *Photo by Michael Gaffney*

Modern-day Black Horse Inn amid the blizzard of 2006. *Photo by John Andrus*

also received a taste for rum and a number of deadly diseases from the settlers, especially small pox, measles, and mumps. The latter caused the death of nearly 90 percent of the Indians.

When there were no more furs to exchange, the remaining Lenape were obliged to trade their rights to the land. Private ownership of land was alien to the Lenape. They believed land was free and to be used by everyone. Bad feelings grew increasingly between the "settlers" and the Indians, so the remnant populations of excluded Lenape opted to move west and north, ending eventually in Oklahoma and Canada. By the eighteenth century, the Lenape were all but gone from Mendham.

Ebenezer Byram's old farmhouse converted to a guest house in 1740— the Black Horse Inn. *Courtesy of Ernie Maw*

The Indians left a few names with us. Iron, originally referred to as black stone, was called "Succasunna." "Roxiticus" meant "a meeting place" and was used to encompass the area that is today Mendham and Ralston.

The First Settlements

As the Indians had come to the area following the streams, so did the new settlers who were able to take advantage of the forests, fruits, and game. The Raritan and Passaic Rivers led them to Mendham. As eloquently stated by Ella Mockridge:

> *Let it be emphasized the Raritan and Passaic rivers rise here in Mendham, the Passaic rises deep under Gunther's Garage and the Raritan from springs feeding Mountain Valley pool. Mendham is the watershed of Morris County. An old saying: "A rain drop split on Hilltop church roof goes half into the Passaic and half into the Raritan and both halves in the same ocean."*

When it was determined that the black stone found in the area was iron, the settlers came in more numbers and began mining. Deposits of coal and lead were also found. Limestone, used in agricultural applications, was also found, and kilns were established in the area.

While there have been recorded Mendham land transactions dating from 1708, the first permanent settlers arrived in the 1720s and made their home along India Brook, just west of Mendham Borough. A settlement was started by David Bainard, an Indian missionary, and Eliab Byram from Yale Divinity School. They conducted services in a log meetinghouse built in 1730.

In 1740 Ebenezer Byram, Eliab's father, moved to Roxiticus from Massachusetts. He was followed by Massachusetts Bay Puritans, who

Left: In 1903 Hilltop Church stands amidst a village with strong agricultural roots. *Courtesy of Michael Smith*

Right: The Tiger Distillery was once located just south of Heather Hill Road. *Courtesy of Ernie Maw*

traveled a road created from a bridle path that connected New York with Easton, Pennsylvania. The halfway point on the trail became a small farmhouse that was converted to an inn by Ebenezer Byram. The inn was called the Black Horse Inn, and the trail, of course, is known today as Main Street. In 1745 Byram requested that John Cary, a Massachusetts neighbor and a carpenter by trade, come to Mendham to help establish a meetinghouse on the site of the present-day Hilltop Church. Perhaps the first instance of gifting to the community can be seen in the November 11, 1745, deed in which Edmon Burnant deeds a certain parcel of land measured off a "red Oke Saplin" to the church for the "Public Worship of God."

It was also in the mid-eighteenth century that Mendham received its name. While today we know just the inn as the Black Horse Tavern, in those days the entire neighborhood was called Black Horse. When the first church was built, Byram changed the name of the neighborhood; he named the settlement "Mendham" from his hometown of Mendham, England. Translated from the Anglo-Saxon, it means "my home."

Life in the Mendhams

Before there was a Mendham Borough, there was a Mendham Township, of which we were a part. The center of the village that had been established in the mid-eighteenth century became the name of one of Morris County's first townships. Mendham Township included all of present-day Mendham Borough, Mendham Township, Chester Township, Chester Borough, and Randolph Township.

Chapter One: Roots of a Village 17

Why applejack?

"There were several reasons why applejack became such a large revenue-producing commodity. Initially, apples flourished better than grains, and Colonial culture was more tolerant toward drinking hard spirits on a regular basis. Also, applejack was cheaper to produce and aged more quickly than grain alcohol. Transportation was not sophisticated enough to carry fresh produce over long distances; therefore, the plentiful apple harvests had to be made into a product that could be transported over time. Applejack was relatively easy to produce, always in demand and nonperishable.

By the late 1600s, hard cider was the most abundant and least expensive beverage in the Northeast. It was used for all occasions, such as weddings, funerals, and political rallies.

Early colonists feared that water carried disease; therefore, it was customary to drink hard cider with breakfast.

In winter when milk was scarce, cider was diluted with water. Babies were given mulled cider at night, which no doubt helped them sleep, and children were fed bread that had been soaked in cider. Living and working conditions were extremely harsh during Colonial times, and hard cider was considered to be good for health and to have restorative powers. In Colonial kitchens hard cider was used to flavor foods, tenderize meat, and moisten cakes."

—Mendham Borough Historical Society: Fall Walking Tour 10-5-97

With the construction of a church on the highest hill in the village, Mendham had two public meeting places: the church and the Black Horse Inn. The village itself was growing along the highway created by the first settlers, and many families, names of which are still known to us today, built their homesteads. The Pitneys, Drakes, Thompsons, Days, and Babbitts were just a few. The first residents were English, Scottish, and Irish.

In those early days, industries were local. Iron ore, limestone, and coal were mined locally, and gristmills and sawmills were started. Fruit was plentiful, apples were abundant, and cider became a readily available beverage. In addition to cider mills, distilleries became prevalent. When passengers on the stagecoach from New York City to Easton, Pennsylvania, asked how long it would be until they reached Mendham, the driver replied, "Not long. I can smell the applejack now."

The impact of the distilleries on life in the village is reflected in the history of the First Presbyterian Church. Ministers had to realize that distilleries were a major source of income to the local farmers, and in those days it was not uncommon for farmers to have their own small private distilleries. Distilleries stayed, and some ministers came and went.

While tending to its life-supporting activities, Mendham did not escape the effects of the Revolutionary War. The village of Mendham played a

Two jugs recently dug from Sharkey's Pond. They are of a type and vintage that would have been used in the production of applejack.

significant part in the revolution by not only providing volunteer troops but by caring for the sick and supplying troops with food and weapons. One township resident, Lebbeus Dod, was reported to have made guns for the Continental Army in his home. According to Ella Mockridge, in 1776, sixty men from Mendham enlisted. Individuals from families such as the Axtells, Riggs, Dods, Thompson, Cooks, Fairchilds, Babbitts, Drakes, Days, Byrams, and Pitneys participated as minutemen and fought in numerous battles.

Mendham villagers also answered the call. In 1780, when Washington's troops located at Jockey Hollow had to endure an extreme winter, villagers rallied with food and supplies to help the soldiers. When Washington's army was quartered in Morristown, a smallpox epidemic broke out. A clinic was set up outside Morristown, and hospitals were established in a barn on the Colonel Drake estate and at Hilltop Church.

After the revolution and during the War of 1812, there were many hard times in the nation and in Mendham. However, as the nineteenth century dawned, the area began changing. Chester Township split off from Mendham Township in 1799, and in 1805 Randolph Township was established. In 1806 a company was chartered to build a turnpike from Phillipsburg/Easton to Morristown. Known as the Washington Turnpike, it passed through Mendham following the older stage route. The regular passage of travelers and goods over the turnpike prompted growth, and Ebenezer Byram's Black Horse Inn grew and changed with the times.

It was also in the early 1800s that a post office was established in the village center. Throughout the nineteenth century, the residents of Mendham Township came into Mendham village to pick up their mail, and they bought the few things they could not make themselves at one or two general stores in the center of town. According to Kate Emmons, local historian, from July 1861 to July 1893, the post office and postmastership moved back and forth across Main Street from Theodore Phoenix to Marius Robinson. The location depended on which political party was in power.

Mendham's population continued to evolve. The Irish in Mendham seemed to blend in with the rest of the initial English and Scottish population, pursuing their crafts and farming alongside descendants of the early settlers. There was, however, another non-English population in Mendham consisting of free blacks and the descendants of slaves who had been in the community since the eighteenth century. While slavery was abolished in New Jersey in 1846, some still approved of the system; and as the Civil War approached, the same tensions that split the country divided Mendham.

Reverend Theodore F. White of the Hilltop Church, a man with strong abolitionist leanings, invited a black man to preach one Sunday. This offended much of the congregation, and the abolitionist supporters broke away to form the Second Presbyterian Church of Mendham. The Second Presbyterian Church was located close to the middle of town, and its members were able to construct a handsome house of worship in 1859. Well after the Civil War, the congregations were reunited, and the second church was demolished around 1901.

Top: Hilltop Cemetery gravestones help relate Mendham's role in the Revolutionary War during the long, cold winters. Later, during one of these storms, the church burned to the ground, as firemen could not climb the icy hill. *Photo by John Andrus*

Bottom: The William Phoenix section of the Hilltop Cemetery. Because of his close ties with the "spirits" (applejack), Phoenix was not allowed to be buried in the cemetery, so he purchased an adjacent plot for his family.

Sharkey House—formerly Restformi, for a time a retirement home for telephone workers—sits on East Main Street streams that become the Raritan and Passaic Rivers. *Courtesy of Don Preziosi*

Robinson's drug shop once was the location for the post office. The post office moved from one side of Main Street to the other, depending on the political party in power. *Courtesy of Ernie Maw*

Changing horses in front of the Sanford Building—another post office location. *Courtesy of Nick Cusano*

> To walk in a town,
> That's almost restored,
> With buildings and scenery,
> And history galore!
> With old firehouses,
> And old engines too!
> Many fine monuments,
> Both old and new.
> The Black Horse Inn,
> Where Washington once slept,
> And the wine in the cellar,
> So perfectly kept.
> The people so friendly,
> And helpful so much,
> For they live in a town,
> With a magic touch.
> They say "hello" here,
> And they say "goodbye" there
> And they are always ready,
> To help and to share.
>
> by,
> Peter Haldopoulos

Left: A poem by Peter Haldopoulos found when the time capsule buried in 1981 was opened.

Right: Vacationers relax on the porch of the Phoenix House among flowers similar to those found in today's planters. *Courtesy of Nick Cusano*

As with other wars, our residents left Mendham to fight in the Civil War, and once again after the war, change hit Mendham. Small industries such as the carriage works were not able to revive. Steam was taking the place of water power, and new modes of transportation, primarily railroads, were making possible the more facile movement of materials throughout the country. Industrialization was replacing the production of many consumer items previously provided by local craftsmen. As a result of all the change, Mendham actually became a more agricultural community, and by the late 1800s farms were abundant.

While Mendham was becoming known as a wonderful summer vacation spot after the Civil War, in the late nineteenth and early twentieth century, millionaires from the New York area built many elaborate country summer estate homes on the south side of town. As much of the Morristown land had already been occupied, they moved farther west to Mendham when the railroad was extended to Bernardsville.

A New Beginning

On May 15, 1906, the final change in the structure of Mendham Township took place. It was determined that Mendham Borough could be bonded only for a distance equal to the gravity flow of water, about a mile in any direction from the center; hence, the borough's boundaries were determined. In order to build a water system, Mendham Borough separated from Mendham Township.

Chapter One: Roots of a Village

Chapter Two
When Grass Grew on Main Street

There was a time when you could play baseball on Main Street. The boys would set their bases, and when a car came along, rather infrequently, the one who saw it first would call "car," and everyone would move off the road to let it pass.

—Johnny Enright IV

When grass grew alongside a dirt road now named Main Street, our predecessors surely would never have dreamed that one day there would be something called a National Historic Register. Even more difficult to fathom might have been that the tiny village of laborers, farmers, and craftsmen would comprise something called the Mendham Borough Historic District and be listed on that register. They would never have dreamed that what they built was formally named a historic district on February 5, 1985, and that the Black Horse Inn, established more than 240 years ago, would be at its center. We are sure, however, that they would be very proud to know that this historic district, consisting of 140 properties, has been well preserved to remind us of the history of the village they built, from its eighteen-century founding to its 1906 incorporation and beyond.

King's Highway was one of the early names for Main Street when it was a dirt road. Well over two hundred years old, at various times in history this road has been called the Washington Turnpike, the Mendham–Morristown Road, and the William Penn Highway. We know it as East and West Main Street, and the county knows it as Route 510. Maps have

View in 1907 west from the crossroads.
Courtesy of Ernie Maw

Celebration of flag raising on the mast of America's Cup challenger *Defender* for the first time, ca. 1912. *Mendham Borough archives*

shown the intersection of King's Highway, Mountain Avenue, and Church Street (Hilltop Road) as the center of the village since the beginning.

The residential, commercial, and religious buildings that have established Mendham's village character are well preserved today. Sixty-one of the eighty-one principal buildings in the district are still standing.

Celebrating at the Crossroads

When grass grew on Main Street, the villagers gathered in the crossroads around a "liberty pole" that displayed the "stars and stripes" in the center of the intersection. These are the crossroads at which we have gathered to share news, celebrate, parade, and wish a safe journey to those leaving us.

According to borough historian Kate Emmons, many early towns had "liberty poles," which were originally erected to rally against Tory enemies during the Stamp Act crisis. After the Revolutionary War, the poles became a symbol of freedom. According to *The Mendhams*, the pole may have originally been located near the Black Horse Inn to celebrate Washington's victory over Cornwallis at Yorktown.

In 1912 a mast of Oregon pine replaced the original liberty pole. Seymour L. Cromwell donated the mast, which is said to have been taken from the 1898 America's Cup yacht *Defender*. In 1918, after lightning struck it, the pole had to be removed—including a forty-foot piece that landed on the Phoenix House. A smaller liberty pole with a light at the base replaced it. The light was subsequently broken when farmer Herbert Bockoven passed too close with a load of hay. He received a bill for damages totaling $13.08.

To Light or Not to Light

To light or not to light . . . the age-old debate . . . or at least the center of Mendham Village debate. From the liberty pole being hit by lightning to Mr. Bockoven's Haytruck incident to the conversion to automated lights, the crossroads have not been without controversy.

In 1930 the borough council began to study whether an automated traffic light was needed in the center of town. In 1931 the New Jersey State Traffic Control Commission wrote the borough, saying it disapproved of an automated signal. It did agree to a manually controlled light that, when not in use, would flash if the council felt it necessary. The signal was installed in 1931 on the base of the old liberty pole.

In 1934 the town again approached the state for an automated light. This time there was heated debate among the council members. Councilman William Cordingley was in extreme opposition. Due to protests by parents, the manual light remained. In 1941 it happened again . . . the Borough Police Committee recommended an overhead traffic light. After much heated debate, the manual traffic light and the safety isle were removed from the center of town. Ironically, Mr. Cordingley, who fought so hard for the removal of the traffic light, was stuck by a car and killed crossing Main Street, yards from where the light had been removed.

In May 1965 the borough council was presented with a petition signed by more than five hundred residents who were in favor of a "stop and go" light. The light was approved by the state in 1966 and installed in 1968, but not without controversy again. The wooden structures that held the lights were referred to as "the gallows," and one morning a dummy was found hanging from them.

New lights have been installed. Now we debate the timing.

—*Through the Years in Mendham Borough,*
Kate Emmons

While the original liberty pole has since been replaced and the flag relocated to make way for traffic lights, our predecessors would be proud to know that the four original buildings of Mendham's crossroads have been preserved and restored through the years.

Ebenezer Byram's Inn

The farmhouse that Ebenezer Byram converted to an inn is the oldest of the four original buildings and has stood for more than 250 years. When Byram purchased it in 1740, the Black Horse Inn was used as a guest house for early travelers and became a popular meeting place, where one could transact business and hear the news of the "outside world." It became a stopping point on the four-day journey from Hacketstown to New York. It later became a tavern, and through the years the original use of the building has been maintained. The exception that is noted is that if you were voting during the great blizzard of 1888, you might have cast a vote at this location.

In the October 17, 1968, *Observer Tribune,* an interview with Miss Elizabeth Phoenix reveals that her great-grandfather, William, owned the Black Horse Inn as well as the Phoenix House. However, local authorities thought he had a monopoly on the sale of spirits and forced him to sell the inn.

> A PART OF THE LIBERTY POLE FROM THE CENTER OF TOWN IS SAID TO REMAIN. WHERE IS IT?
>
> ANSWER: ELLA MOCKRIDGE'S BACK YARD

While the building itself has evolved through the years, the original structure is still evident. Remodeled in the early nineteenth century, the structure's porch was enclosed in the 1980s. At one time, the inn had paired front doors, a typical feature of early inns. One door led directly into the bar and the other into the inn—the proper entrance for ladies. A building on the site that was once a shed where horses rested and then cars were parked became the original pub, which was later expanded to the current building. The structure had previously been renovated to house a dress shop and an antiques store. Many Mendhamites also remember the "Foxes Den" that was located in the basement section now occupied by a retail store.

According to Kate Emmons, the Fornaro family relates that after they purchased the inn in 1958, they discovered a false floor in one of the bedrooms where containers as large as five gallons could be stored. Carpeting and a trap door hid the location. In the basement, they found a coal bin with a false bottom. This, coupled with old liquor bottles, provided evidence of life during the prohibition era.

This hand-drawn sketch of the Black Horse Inn in 1976 Michas calendar noted, "Some historians say the town of Mendham was once known as 'black horse' but was changed to Mendham by its founding father, Byram." Artist: G. William Michas. *Courtesy of the Michas family*

The Phoenix House Roadhouse

Around 1800 a building was constructed across the street from the Black Horse Inn to serve as a girl's seminary. Acquired by William Phoenix for $3,500, successive generations of the Phoenix family operated it as a general store, tavern, and inn for almost one hundred years. The building offered good food and lodging to travelers along the Washington Turnpike, and it helped make Mendham a popular summer resort. From 1820 until after WWI, the Phoenix House roadhouse was a Mecca for vacationing gentry seeking bucolic views, peace and quiet, and American-style fine dining. Well known guests at the Phoenix Hotel included Civil War Generals Abner Doubleday and Leroy Stone, Leroy Stone's daughter and her British nobleman husband, Lord Monson, and the son of the "Star-Spangled Banner" author, Francis Scott Key.

The Phoenix House is a registered historic American building and an architectural legacy of the borough and the township. It is senior of the only three brick Federal-style edifices that masons in the Mendhams built from handmade Chester brick. In 1838 Mendham builder/architect Aaron Hudson designed and constructed a Greek-revival two-story portico and colonnaded porch on the northern and eastern aspects of the house. Thus, the house became the architectural treasure we see today. The Historic American Building Survey's Federal Advisory Committee recognized it as worthy of preservation for future generations, and detailed plans and drawings of the building are on record in the Library of Congress in Washington, D.C.

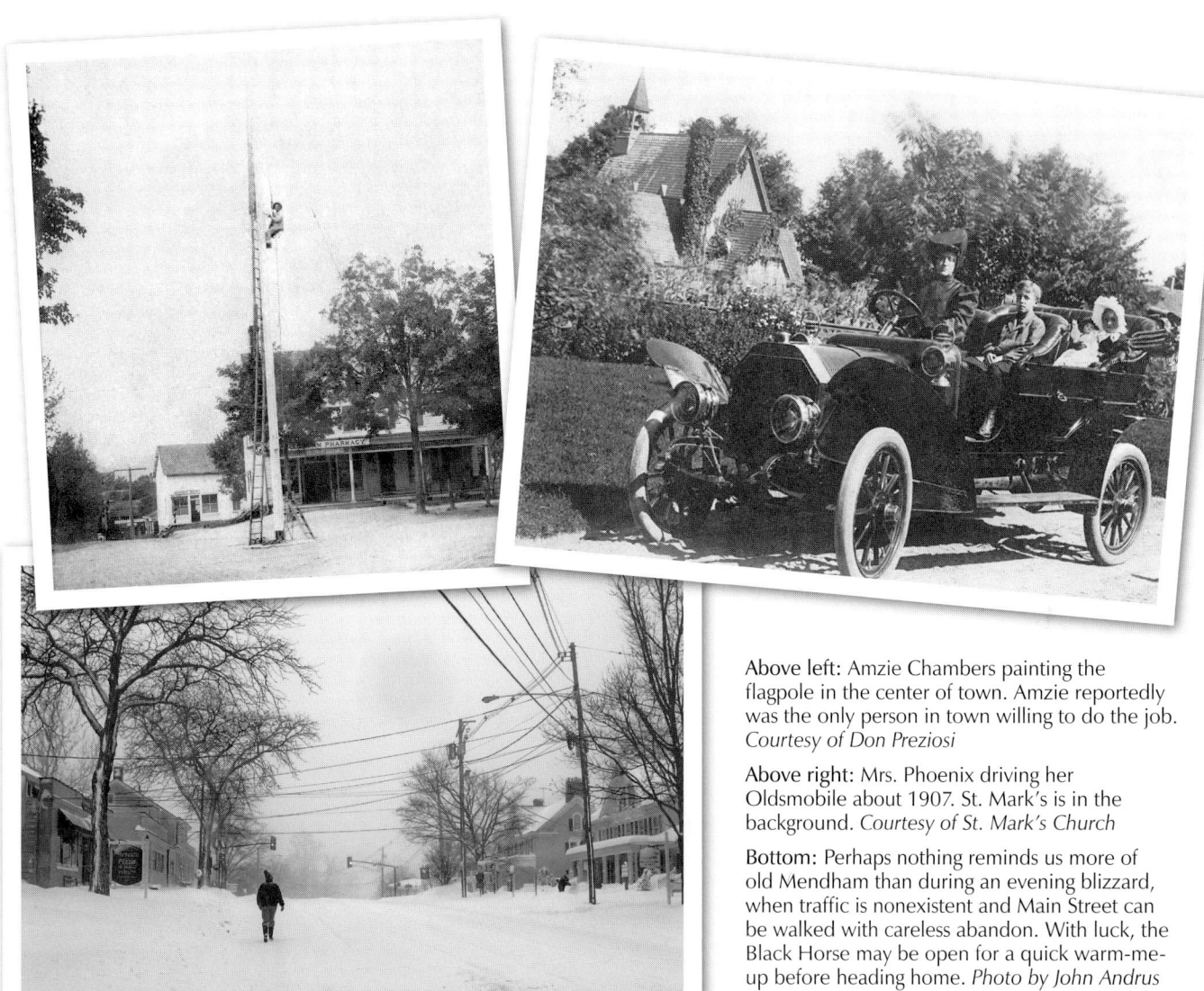

Above left: Amzie Chambers painting the flagpole in the center of town. Amzie reportedly was the only person in town willing to do the job. *Courtesy of Don Preziosi*

Above right: Mrs. Phoenix driving her Oldsmobile about 1907. St. Mark's is in the background. *Courtesy of St. Mark's Church*

Bottom: Perhaps nothing reminds us more of old Mendham than during an evening blizzard, when traffic is nonexistent and Main Street can be walked with careless abandon. With luck, the Black Horse may be open for a quick warm-me-up before heading home. *Photo by John Andrus*

Township residents Senator and Mrs. Arthur Whitney, with others, purchased the Phoenix House and its furnishings in 1919 from William N. Phoenix. From that time on, it was used as a teashop, antiques store, and dress shop. In 1929 the Whitneys acquired full title. Aware of the building's historical significance, Whitney and his wife donated the vacated mansion to the people of Mendham Borough in June 1938 "in order that it might be preserved for future generations in as nearly its original condition as would be consistent with its use." Not wanting recognition for their generosity, the Whitneys stipulated that the building be known as "The Phoenix House, belonging to the People of Mendham." Since then, many groups, including the Mendham Borough Historical Society and Mendham Garden Club, have used the house as a meeting place. The Police Department was initially located on the first floor and later in the basement for many years, and since 1960 the building has housed borough offices. A million-dollar historic preservation of the building was completed in 2005.

Had we been enjoying a celebration at the liberty pole, we could have stopped for a moment on the corner of Main and Hilltop by the Phoenix

> *If one was to enter the Black Horse Inn and ask Ebenezer Byram for a "horn of gunpowder," an "essence of lockjaw," a "hedge-hog quill" or a "blue-fish hooks," what would one expect to get?*
>
> *Answer: Jersey lightning applejack*

Chapter Two: When Grass Grew on Main Street

House and looked down the street. Picture, if you will, that after the Civil War, the two-story porch on the Phoenix House was connected to the building next door.... The building, which today is a clothing store and apartment, was at one time the Phoenix House Annex, built to accommodate the house's increasing number of guests. Across the street is the Wilder House, at 6 Hilltop Road, also owned by the Phoenix Wilder family and used for extra hotel rooms. What was once a barn and paint shop in the rear of the Wilder House was near ruin in 1950 but repaired and converted to specialty shops in 1970.

In the latter 1800s, William Phoenix's daughter had taken over the Phoenix Hotel Road House, and it was now a genteel boardinghouse. However, if we looked closely, we might have noticed a woman at the side door of the Phoenix House on Hilltop Road. Miss Julia, the proprietor of the Phoenix House after the Civil War, could reach the annex through the side door. Inside "Miss Julia's Room" she handled supplier accounts and ensured work was being completed in the Phoenix House yard. Stories also relate that applejack was sold from the side door.

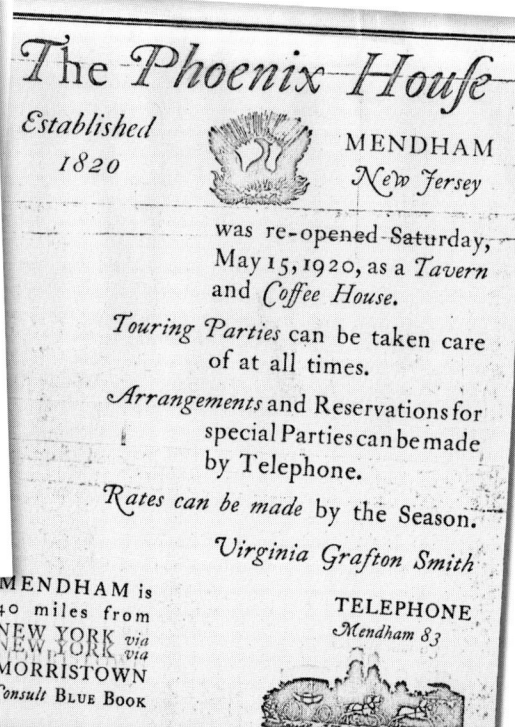

Top left: Looking south on Hilltop, one can see the connecting porches from the Phoenix House to the annex next door. *Mendham Borough archives*

Top right: The Phoenix House, marketed for its location as a vacation destination for New Yorkers, was used in 1920 as a tavern and coffeehouse. *Mendham Borough archives*

Bottom: Miss Julia's Room is a small brick addition to the main Phoenix House. The window to the right was a door that connected to a dining annex, now removed, in the rear of the building. *Mendham Borough Library archives*

Left: Phoenix House entranceway—architectural beauty and simplicity before becoming the borough administrative offices. *Mendham Borough Library archives*

Right: In 1938 one could have an ice cream soda at Robinson's while waiting for a prescription. Reginald Robinson, pharmacist, and Kate Emmons, clerk and future borough historian, would greet you. *Mendham Borough Library archives*

Multipurpose Drug Shop

Robinson's Drug Shop was built around 1870 and was then known as the Garabrant–Robinson General Store. Marius Robinson purchased the drug business from Cornelius Aller, who had been a proprietor of a drugstore business in the building now known as the Pastime Club. After the death of Marius Robinson in 1900, his son, Leo Robinson, became the proprietor. In 1923 Leo's son, Reginald R. Robinson, joined his father and became the third generation to occupy the building.

In combination with the drugstore business of many years, the building was also the location of the borough's first telephone service in the 1930s, served as a post office, and housed the auxiliary button for the borough's fire alarm. It also served the borough as a location for the payment of water bills and the issuance of hunting and fishing licenses. Residents could conduct banking business at this location when the Morristown Building and Loan Association representative arrived once a month. The building was even a favorite ice cream parlor.

General Store

The last remaining building in our crossroads was built as a general store on the corner of Hilltop and West Main Street. It was a partnership of William Phoenix and his uncle, Ed Sanford. Thus, to many, the building became known as the Sanford Building, and the business, Phoenix and Sanford's. While today the building is connected to the structure directly adjacent to it on Hilltop Road, when built, they were detached. The home located directly around the corner on Hilltop Road was the home of William Phoenix. Through the years, the Sanford-Phoenix building has housed retail stores and a restaurant.

> *For what act is John Gilmer Speed known?*
>
> *Answer: He shot himself in 1909 while staying in the Phoenix House.*

Chapter Two: When Grass Grew on Main Street

Top left: St. Mark's Rectory on East Main Street once housed Bretherton's Plumbing Store. *Courtesy of Ernie Maw*

Top right: Freeman Building. From west of the center, a 2006 photo shows little change in the building structures. *Photo by Michael Gaffney*

Bottom left: Freeman Brothers Blacksmith and Carriage Shop was located next to their store. The site evolved into an automobile service station in the 1920s. *Courtesy of Ernie Maw*

Bottom right: George Lounsbury delivering groceries for his brother, Herb. *Courtesy of Honey Belton*

Shopping the Historic Village

Commercial buildings in Mendham's Historic District reflect the town's history as a local center for business. Some structures were converted to business uses from houses; others were constructed originally for commercial use. If we could tour the historic district absent a timeframe, we would see that the commercial buildings in the village through the years included hardware stores, general stores, shoemaker shops, dry goods and grocery stores, butcher shops, and ice cream parlors. We've already visited the pharmacy, the inns and the general store. Mendham even had a coach factory in operation prior to 1860, but the business did not survive after the Civil War. There was also a tannery north of West Main Street, which supplied leather for harnesses.

In 1902 a shopping trip could have been started at the "Freeman Brothers" store, a new three-story structure built on West Main Street. Imagine entering one of the largest structures in town at the time to purchase dry goods and groceries. Residents living above the store would have seen us through windows that had been salvaged from the former Second Presbyterian Church. En route to the next destination, we would have passed Freeman's Garage and Blacksmith Shop next door. The garage became the site of an automobile service station in the 1920s and today is the home of a cleaners and nail salon.

Telephone Service

The first telephone was installed in the Borough in 1892 on the rear wall near the cigar counter of the Mendham Pharmacy, today Robinsons Drug Shop. It was connected to a switchboard in Morristown, New Jersey. As it was the only phone in town, anyone wishing to use the phone had to come to this location, and people needed to be found and brought to the location to receive their calls. At that time, a young Leo Robinson may have been called out of school to deliver the messages.

About 1898 a very small switchboard was installed in the drug store just inside the prescription department. The switchboard was operated by the pharmacist. In 1900 there were only three telephones in the Borough. Through the years the switchboard moved to several private homes, and by 1931 we had a four person switchboard. By 1960 Mendham joined the more up to date dial system. The present colonial brick building located on East Main Street serves both Mendham Borough and Mendham Township.

The Borough has also adapted to the times, by permitting the installation of a cell tower located at St. John Baptist. Long discussions with the Board of Adjustment led to the design that to many has been recognized only as a bell tower.

—Through the Years in Mendham Borough, pages 104–106

While our predecessors might have questioned our needs for nail salons, cleaners, and other service businesses, hardware and plumbing were key needs to them. There were several plumbing shops at various locations through the years. The Groendykes had a plumbing business on West Main Street in what today is a business office that many of us recognize as having a strong resemblance to a castle. There was also a plumbing shop behind 2 and 4 West Main Street in the 1890s that became a barbershop in 1932, and ultimately was renovated to serve as a residence. In addition, one could obtain plumbing and hardware in the Sanford Building and in the building that today is the rectory for St. Mark's Church.

There would have been food choices on our shopping trip as well. One could stop at Quimby's for an ice cream cone, or could pick up the meat for dinner at the Coghlan butchers before heading home. The location of Quimby ice cream parlor is today a retail business, and the icebox used by the Coghlan butchers those many years ago remains in working condition in the Colonial Pantry. Meat could also be purchased in the small butcher's building that today is a dentist's office on Mountain Avenue. With a livestock dealer located on Main

E. Sanford and Company, located at the corner of Hilltop Road and East Main Street, served as the general store ca. 1880. In the early 1900s it was Coghlan's Plumbing, and in the 1940s it was Moeri's Store. *Courtesy of Ruth Smith*

Chapter Two: When Grass Grew on Main Street

Top left: Office space today, 12 West Main Street was home to the Village Food Shop. The Village Food Shop was operated by William and Mickey Fagan, who obtained a liquor license and moved to the Village Shopping Center in the 1960s. *Courtesy of Don Preziosi*

Top right: Real-life John Quimby and Michael Coghlan outside the store on West Main Street in the early 1900s. *Courtesy of Don Quimby*

Bottom: The oak refrigerator in Coghlan's. Today it remains at the Colonial Pantry. *Courtesy of Sam Vacchiano*

Street, one would have expected fresh meat in the town. Later in time, one could have visited the Village Food Shop, located at 12 West Main Street.

If pastries tempted you, at one point in time baked goods, ice cream, and popsicles could have been purchased at the Annex Bakery, also run by a Quimby and located across from the post office on Hilltop Road. One's table setting could be completed by buying flowers at the Quimby Florist Greenhouses on New Street.

Shoes could also be picked up at the shoemaker shop, but from which shop in what timeframe…. In the mid- to late 1800s, there was a shoemaker shop located next to 25 East Main Street. One of our longtime residents, Pete Cillo, relates his story of having to go help his grandfather in the shop every day after school. While the shop is now removed, 25 East Main Street was home to Gibraltar Bank, and then, for more than two decades, Eric Sellin's fine restaurant, Mariques. It is soon to be converted back to a bank. According to research completed by Charles Topping of the historical society, the building was originally used as a bed, breakfast, and supper house for skilled masons and artisans who came to Mendham looking for work at the turn of the century.

Another shoe shop was located on Mountain Avenue. Used by Henry Drake in the early 1800s and David Carlisle, a shoemaker in the 1880s, the home was converted to a residence in the 1960s. The current owners, Mr. and Mrs. Tufariello, discovered the original markings on the building during renovation.

While some continuation of original uses in our commercial buildings has been a key to preservation, change of use, although altering some structures quite significantly, has kept buildings standing that might otherwise have come down. The hardware, plumbing, and general stores have been replaced by nail and hair salons, retail clothing and jewelry stores, offices, and apartments to meet our current needs, but the buildings and their history have been left for us to enjoy and remember.

Residential Preservation

Grass still grows on Main Street, Mountain, Hilltop, New, and Prospect Streets. The houses in the historic district are predominantly single-family and two-story, set back from the street with modest front yards. The streets are shaded, and regularly spaced oaks and elms add to the character to the streets. Most of the homes are frame, some with their original clapboard or shingle siding. Many have had aluminum or vinyl siding put on in recent years.

Varying in architecture, some are still known by the name of their original owners. The residential building thought to be the oldest within the historic district is the Daniel Babbitt/Silas Thompson House on the corner of West Main and New Streets.

Styles of the homes and architectural details incorporated in our historic district range from New England style to East Jersey cottage (Cape Cod) to Federal to Greek Revival to Italianate to today's more modern styles. Given an economic downturn in the latter half of the nineteenth century, there was not much building, and therefore, there is not a great deal of Victorian architecture in the village. At the turn of the century, there was a major building boom in Mendham. Fully one-third of the structures in the historic district were built between 1890 and 1930.

While we recognize the homes that line East and West Main Street as part of the historic past, some homes on New and Prospect Streets share a long history. Prospect Street was originally known as Seminary Street, and New Street was so named because it was the second street laid out in the village's center. There were no other streets laid out prior to the incorporation of the borough in 1906.

Top: As portrayed by the artist, there apparently is more to the Quimby/Coghlan story than ice cream and meat. *Courtesy of Don Quimby*

Bottom: While renovating their home at 11 Mountain Avenue, the Tufariellos found siding that indicated its former use. *Courtesy of Dominique and Michael Tufariello*

Worthy of Dessert

"When sidewalks were first proposed in the village in 1925, many residents were very concerned about the fate of the trees. Ella Mockridge, the woman responsible for starting the Garden Club, brought the residents' concerns to the town council. After construction was completed and the trees remained, the happy residents treated the council members to ice cream and cake."

—Mendham Borough Historical Society: Fall Walking Tour 10-5-97

The Historical Society Walking Tour

Each fall the Mendham Borough Historical Society treats grade school students to a walking tour of Mendham history and architecture. It's a short walk, as it has been said that one can view an example of almost every architectural style in Mendham by walking Hilltop, New, and Prospect Streets.

11 Hilltop Road—Aaron Hudson built this as his own home around 1840, probably changing the columns to square piers for ease of construction. This projecting front portico with the bold triangular pediment is classic Greek Revival. In contrast to the classical lines of the Greek style, Hudson added a second floor window with a gothic arch and lattice work. Like the Phoenix House, he wanted this house to be noticed.

17 Hilltop Road—Built around 1800 and known as the Doctor's House because it was occupied by doctors from 1850 to 1908, this house also is a two-story, three-bay with a side hall.

2 Prospect Street—The Fairchild–Rankin House was built around 1800 and does not fit into any common category. It's square with a pyramid-shaped roof and two massive chimneys.

3 Prospect Street—The Robinson House was erected in the early 1930s and faithfully reproduces a typical one-and-a-half-story, three-bay cottage. It is a replica of a Williamsburg house and is the most authentic Colonial reproduction house in the village.

Top: 11 Hilltop Road. *Photo by Michael Gaffney*

Bottom: 17 Hilltop Road. *Photo by Michael Gaffney*

6 and 8 Prospect Street—Number 6 is the William Rankin House, built in the 1860s. Both are fine examples of one of the most vernacular building types: two-and-a-half-story, five-bay house with central door and gable roof. The origins of this style are the Georgian period, which was more formal and characterized by symmetrical proportions.

Top left: 2 Prospect Street about 1870. *Courtesy of Ernie Maw*

Top right: 2 Prospect Street. *Photo by Michael Gaffney*

Middle left: 3 Prospect Street. *Photo by Michael Gaffney*

Middle right: 6 Prospect Street. *Photo by Michael Gaffney*

Bottom: 7 and 9 Prospect Street. *Photo by Michael Gaffney*

7 and 9 Prospect Street—Built by Italian masons who emigrated to work on the mansions in the area. These masons built their own homes in a "modern style." Built around 1915, they are masonry finished with stucco.

12 Prospect Street—The De Groot House is a Mendham variation of the typical Georgian five-bay house.

Mansion, left side of Prospect—Built in 1912 in the Colonial Revival style for Dr. George De Groot. The elements are designed for emphasis and to

Chapter Two: When Grass Grew on Main Street 35

be impressive, such as the semicircular porch with two-story Ionic columns, elliptical fanlights over the windows, and round arched dormers in the attic.

Cube House, New Street—The Nicholas House was built in 1840. It is considered to be high-style Greek Revival with strong horizontal and vertical lines. A different style from Aaron Hudson.

3 and 5 New Street—Small "working man" houses built in the late 1800s, they are loosely categorized as Victorian but lack the extensive exterior details.

8 New Street—The Quimby House is Queen Anne style from the early 1900s. It has many elaborate flourishes, such as scalloped shingles, bay windows, colored glass window margins, and ornate window brackets.

Corner New and Main—The Daniel Babbitt/Silas Thompson House is the oldest building in the historic district, but may not be the oldest house in town. It has all the characteristics of an east Jersey cottage.

14 West Main Street—The McMurtry House was built in 1891 and is the most ornate Victorian in the village. At one time, Kate Emmons lived here with her family.

Top left: 12 Prospect Street, old. *Mendham Borough archives*

Top right: 12 Prospect Street. *Photo by Michael Gaffney*

Bottom left: Mansion on Prospect. *Photo by Michael Gaffney*

Bottom right: The Cube House on New Street. *Photo by Michael Gaffney*

Left: 8 New Street. *Photo by Michael Gaffney*

Top right: Daniel Babbitt/Silas Thompson House. *Photo by John Andrus*

Bottom right: 14 West Main Street, McMurtry House. *Photo by Michael Gaffney*

Churches in the Historic District

Mendham was originally begun as a settlement built around a church, originally referred to as a "meeting house." The people met and made all the important community decisions. Four churches, ranging from more than 150 to nearly 250 years old, currently have their homes in the historic district: Hilltop First Presbyterian Church, the Methodist Church, St. Joseph's Catholic Church, and St. Mark's Episcopal Church. These four churches can be seen to the south, east, and west as we stand at the crossroads.

Hilltop First Presbyterian Church

Look to the sky when walking up Hilltop or Talmage Roads, and you'll see the steeple of Hilltop Church, the oldest established church in the borough, sitting on a hill to the south of the crossroads. Hilltop Church's structure and location as we know it today has undergone several changes through the years until evolving into the structure that greets us today. Those who visit the churchyard are struck by the extent to which the history of Mendham stands before them. Graves date from the Revolutionary War era, and one cannot help but notice familiar names of many of our founding families. The church on the hilltop remains a beacon searching to remember Mendham's past.

While now located in the center of the borough, the church has evolved from the small log meetinghouse originally established at "Rocksiticus" in 1738. That original meetinghouse, located near the Ralston General Store, was known as "Gods Barn" and consisted of a cabin with one door and two

Chapter Two: When Grass Grew on Main Street 37

Students in Hilltop Cemetery at memorial gravestone for the twenty-seven Revolutionary War soldiers who died of smallpox in 1777. Rear l-r: D. Vallacchi, B. DeGraff, K. White, B. Battaglia, T. Brady, E. Wellman, M. Scheid, T. Thurlow. Front: M. Frisch, T. Gemberling, M. Sinzer, E. Morall. *Photo by Jenny Gemberling*

According to Hilltop's Reverend Cox, how many distilleries were owned by members of his parish?

Answer: Twenty

windows without glass. It had neither lighting nor heat, neither belfry nor steeple. After seeing to the construction and successful operation of the Black Horse Inn, Ebenezer Byram was the impetus to have his friend, John Cary, construct a new edifice on top of the hill where the current "hilltop" church now stands. The fact that Ebenezer's son, Eliab, was the minister of the Spartan meetinghouse may have influenced his decision. It was dedicated in 1745 and became the center of town life at the time. The building was a traditional, square-shaped meetinghouse in the old New England tradition.

As you stroll up the hill toward the church on a beautiful day, think about how the Mendham area served as a main supply source for the Continental Army in the area, and, at Jockey Hollow, how many of the church members served during the revolution and how the church served as a hospital for troops during the smallpox outbreak of 1776. Visit the cemetery and the graves of twenty-seven soldiers taken by smallpox. Not far away is the grave of Reverend Thomas Lewis, who became ill while tending the sick and who died in August 1777.

Through the years, the church leaders faced the economic pressures of Mendham. Fundraising changed from the sale of pews and seats to subscription and back to the sale of seats. Church records show members being prosecuted for nonpayment of subscriptions. It was even difficult to raise the $400 salary of the Reverend Amzi Armstrong, who served the church for twenty years, during which time he doubled the congregation to 260 and led the fundraisings for a much larger church building with steeple, balcony, and gallery at a cost of $6,000.

Ministers after Reverend Armstrong were confronted with a different economic reality. Reverend Samuel Cox. who, despite a 50 percent increase in salary, resigned abruptly, stating, "Their (his congregation) great monster enemy was inebriety." He was

Hilltop Church at night. *Michael Gaffney*

38   *Reflections on a Community:* Mendham Borough ∽ The Centennial 1906–2006

My Mother

By Joan Snyder Palmer

My mother, Bertha Yeager Snyder, was born in 1913 and died in 1998. She went to the one-room Union School from fifth through eighth grade. She walked a mile to school and lived on a farm on Mosle Road. She went early to turn up the stove so the school would be warmer when the children arrived. At the spring, she got water for the school. A new teacher came every year from Montclair Normal School. In nice weather, they ate lunch picnic-style down by the river.

When my mother graduated on June 16, 1927, she received a book [containing] the Declaration of Independence, the Constitution of the United States, and the Constitution of New Jersey. I still have the book. The year 1926 would have been the 150th anniversary of the Declaration of Independence.

In 1927 my mother went to Mendham High School. They went by bus, except when the snow was heavy. Then they went via Babbit's horse and sleigh.

About ten years ago, she told me this story—about the special gravestone in the back of Hilltop Presbyterian Church that was erected in 1927, almost eighty years ago. The gravestone says:

> In Memoriam AD1777
> In the Old Church on the Present Site
> A Camp Hospital for the American Army
> Twenty-Seven Soldiers Died of Small Pox and
> Lie Buried Here
> Erected 1927

In 1927 all schoolchildren in Morris County each donated 10 cents, and that is how the stone was bought. My mother was fourteen and a freshman at Mendham High School. She said she was so proud to donate her dime. It was a special memory for her, and when she told me about it, she remembered it like it was yesterday.

---

succeeded by Reverend Philip Courtland Hay. Unfortunately, Reverend Hay soon faced the facts of life—distilleries were a major source of income to the local farmers, and not all product was exported for consumption by others. Hay led vigorous attacks against those members who had distilleries. The attacks failed, and he was dismissed after a very short stay of service.

Perhaps lightning does not strike twice, but you would have had a difficult time convincing the Hilltop Church parishioners of the mid-1800s. Picture an intermission in a day-long service in 1815, when lightning from a sudden thunderstorm struck a tree next to the manse, damaging the building and killing a parishioner, Martha Drake. Twenty years later, on February 17, 1835, the church burned to the ground. By November of the same year, it was replaced, only to face another fire on February 20, 1859. Although there may have been opportunity to control the second fire, the night was teeming with sleet and freezing rain, and the ground was so slick that even on their hands and knees, firefighters could not make the climb up the hill. But once again the congregation persevered, and a new structure was completed early in 1860. Aaron Hudson's design for the current building was based on Boston's North Church.

> DR. JOSEPH S. DE GROOT IS BURIED IN THE ONLY MAUSOLEUM IN HILLTOP CEMETERY. WHO ACCOMPANIES HIM?
>
> ANSWER: HIS WIFE AND CAT

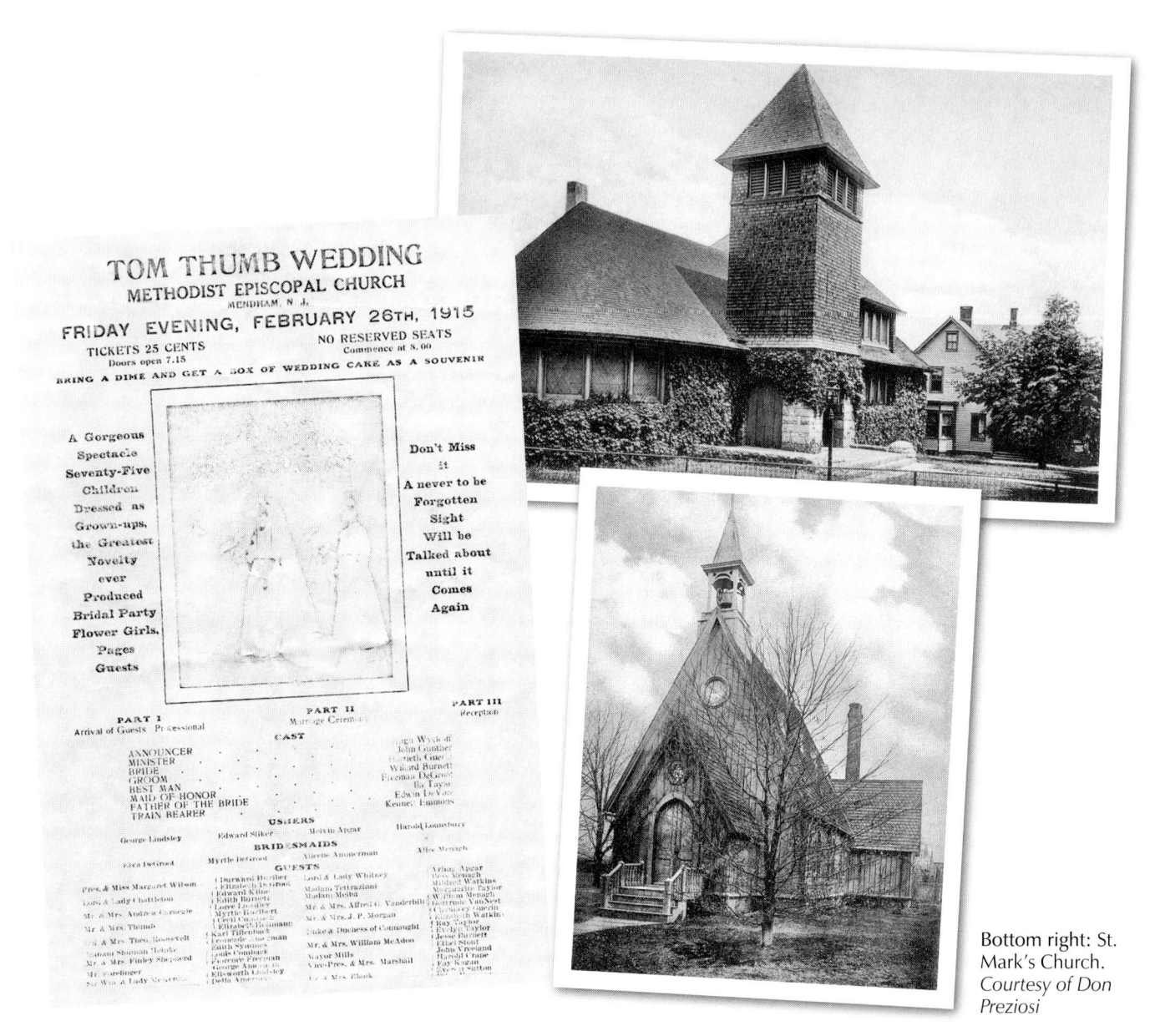

Left: Entertainment at Methodist Episcopal church, 1915—a "Tom Thumb wedding." *Courtesy of Mrs. De Vore*

Top right: Methodist Episcopal Church. *Courtesy of Don Preziosi*

Bottom right: St. Mark's Church. *Courtesy of Don Preziosi*

After the turmoil of the Civil War era, the church survived and remained a center of influence within the borough. As costs rocketed after World War II, fundraising became a social event, and a Friday night turkey dinner was instituted. A 1952 note shows the dinners required some 479 pounds of turkey from Pitney Farms; coleslaw was to be prepared from scratch; and 84 pies were baked for dessert. There were two seatings as well as take-out. The price for dinner—$3.50.

As the century progressed, one Hilltop's most memorable ministers arrived, Reverend Bob Phillips. During his tenure, the children's sermon was instituted, a candlelight Christmas Eve service began, and the Boy and Girl Scouts made frequent use of the church facilities. Reverend Phillips was an active fire and first aid department member until he died prematurely in 1984.

Mendham Methodist Church

It was in the mid-nineteenth century that another congregation established itself in Mendham. Their church is to the east of the crossroads and would develop an interesting history of uses.

In 1828 the seeds for a Methodist Church were planted when Daniel Mullen invited a Mendham preacher, Reverend Lovell, to speak to his friends and relatives at the Ralston Schoolhouse. Inspired by the reverend, a local industrialist, Ingham Kinsey, offered his cotton factory as a place of worship. Recognized as a church by the Philadelphia conference in 1829, the parish was served by an alternating circuit of preachers. During this time, the congregation depended heavily on its members to perform the duties of a permanent minister, and as the membership grew, they considered funding a church building. Opposition by the Presbyterian congregation was noted, but the current site was purchased from Elias Babbitt in 1833.

A small frame church, about thirty-five feet square, was dedicated the same year, and the first permanent minister, Reverend Charles Whitecar, came in 1838 to serve some eighty-nine members. Later in the nineteenth century, "union schools" were run by Methodists, and about 1863 there were funds available to purchase the parsonage on West Main Street. The house remains standing today.

The church became incorporated in 1881 under the name of Mendham Methodist Episcopal Church, but in only ten years a new building was needed. The old church building was purchased by the town (township at the time) to become its municipal building. Until the new quarters were built, it was located in front of, and served as, the town firehouse.

The new edifice was made of stone quarried from William Bedell's farm and hauled to the building site by church members. Opposition no longer forthcoming, services during the construction were held at the First Presbyterian Church. Over the years, the church has been updated, and extensive remodeling took place in 1959. Significantly, ivy, which had covered the building, was removed so the craftsmanship of the forefathers would be visible, and for more than 175 years the building has retained many of its architectural features.

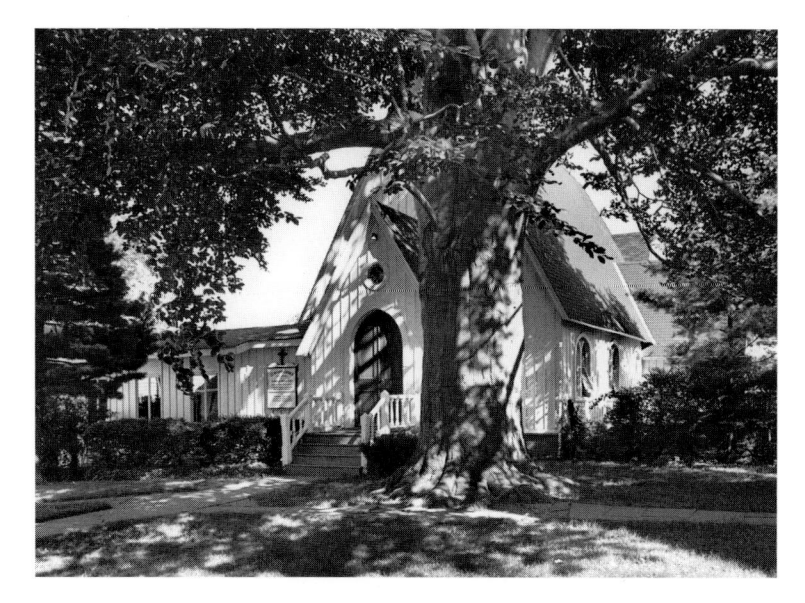

Top: St. Mark's after the addition. *Mendham Borough archives*

Bottom: Christmas pageant at St. Mark's Church, 1983.

St. Mark's Episcopal Church

Across the street from the Methodist Church, St. Mark's Episcopal Church was built in 1872. Reverend Merritt of St. Peter's Church in Morristown began holding services in Mendham in 1867 on an intermittent basis. Regular services began at Mrs. Dodd's School in 1869, and by 1872 Ethelbert Talbot began the process of constructing a church. Reverend Levi Johnston became the first minister in 1881; he not only retained the position for thirty-one

Top left: Michas sketch of St. Joseph's Church completed in 1975. G. William Michas. *Courtesy of the Michas family*

Top right: St. Joseph's before being rebuilt. *Courtesy of Don Preziosi*

Bottom: Father Lasch leads the line dancing at a St. Joseph's event. *Courtesy of Barbara Nelson*

years but is credited with purchasing the rectory property in 1886 and donating it to the parish. The church property was donated by John Van Vorst six years later. The new church was designed by architect Richard Upjohn in a Gothic design style.

Of interest is that from 1872 to 1908, St. Mark's was often closed during the winter because much of the congregation consisted of city residents who only vacationed in Mendham. In 1956, St. Mark's officially became a parish with Reverend Elwood Boggess serving as it first rector.

Despite extensive damage caused by a fire in 1944 that gutted the sacristy and body of the church building, sacred vessels and vestments were removed to safety. A new pipe organ was added in 1964, and St. Mark's remains a part of the Anglican-Episcopal Church.

St. Joseph's Church

Completed in 1859, St. Joseph's Church stands but three buildings to the west of the crossroads. The late 1800s brought prosperity to the Northeast, and with it, the need for more parishes to serve the spiritual needs of the growing Catholic population of southwestern Morris County. St. Joseph's Parish in Mendham was established first as a "mission" of St. Vincent Parish in Madison in 1857 to serve the needs of approximately fifty Catholic families in the Mendham area. Soon after its designation as a mission, construction began

Renovation Surprises

The construction of a new edifice attached to a seventy-year-old church and a thirty-year-old parish center is no easy task. Many unforeseen complications resulted in a hiatus of three months before actual construction began on St. Joseph's Church. A sense of humor always helps in the midst of unanticipated construction woes. Only those who have undertaken the construction of a home can appreciate the delicate balance between dream and reality.

During the demolition of ancillary rooms adjacent to the church and gymnasium, a water line feed to the furnace in the basement of the old church was accidentally severed. The break apparently occurred without notice on the day before Thanksgiving. Bright and early on the following Saturday morning as Father Lasch walked across the church parking lot, he noticed what appeared to be smoke seeping out of the eves of the old wooden church. As he entered the building, he saw it was filled with dark smoke. Running back to the rectory, he called the fire department, and within minutes, every firefighter in Mendham had arrived. Father Lasch thought, "For sure, they will think I was trying to burn the church down to make room for the new!"

The firemen quickly traced the source of the black soot to the boiler in the basement. The lack of water and the malfunction of the failsafe turn-off had resulted in an explosion in the fire chamber of the furnace, which had overheated for lack of water. After everyone took a deep breath of relief, construction proceeded without interruption, but not without the pastor having to fill the boiler twice a day by hand.

One additional glitch amused onlookers as they watched a large crane lift the aluminum replica of the original eight hundred-pound wood steeple. As the crane lowered the steeple, it became clear that the anchors on the new steeple were a few inches off, and it had to be returned to Cambellsville, Kentucky, for corrective measures. The second attempt two months later was successful.

—Fr. Kenneth Lasch

on a church. Designed by local Mendham architect Aaron Hudson, it was of wood frame construction in the Neo-Gothic style. Some have referred to the little church as the "poor man's Gothic cathedral." The church was completed in 1859 at a cost of $650 and dedicated by Dean McNulty in 1860, making it the oldest Roman Catholic Church in the Diocese of Paterson. In 1874 the Mission of St. Joseph was granted the status of its own title as an independent parish with the appointment of a full-time pastor.

The proportional increase in the Catholic population during the late seventies and into the eighties created a need for the expansion of parish facilities. A feasibility study for the construction of a new church was initiated in 1985. With the assistance of a historic preservation architect, V. S. Riggi, plans were drawn for a new church, school expansion, and parish house. Groundbreaking took place on April 25, 1987, and the structure was dedicated in 1989.

St. Joseph's Feast at the Sisters of Christian Charity.

Evolution of a Library

The borough has expanded to meet the current needs of our residents while attempting to preserve its past for the future. A prime example of another common thread in our community, the contributions of our citizens, can be found in the history of the library. Located at various times in different buildings in the historic district, the first library was established in 1797.

In 1912, if we had wanted to visit the library, we would have visited the original section of St. Mark's Parish House. Ten years later, we would have visited the library at a small building on Mountain Avenue directly behind Robinson's Drug Shop. In the early days, we would have bid a good afternoon to Miss Eunice Gunther (Mrs. Richard Clark), the first trained librarian, who traveled from Newark to serve the library until 1920.

When located at St. Mark's parish house, the Mendham Library Association, formed by a group known as the Literary Club, was managing the library. About one thousand volumes would have been available for schoolchildren as well as adults. The membership fee was $1 with a lending fee of 25 cents per book. The Book and Thimble Club was formed at about the same time. A member of the club read to the group as the other members sewed articles to be sold at their yearly bazaar to raise funds for maintaining the library. This group continued their efforts for the library until 1933.

Today the Friends of the Mendham Free Public Library, a volunteer group, are very actively raising funds for the benefit of the library operations. They have held a variety of fundraisers, including house tours, jazz events, and book sales. The library profits from the efforts of a dedicated core of volunteers. On any given day, there are at least one or two volunteers in the library working at the circulation desk, stacking books on the shelves, answering the telephone, and performing the many activities that make the library a vital and interesting place to be. Community activities sponsored by the library reach all ages. There is story time for children, book discussion groups for young and old alike, art exhibits, and programs of current interest topics.

Guest reader from the Madison police reads at children's hour. *Mendham Borough Library archives*

The history of the library built on Hilltop Road in 1920 once again serves as an example of people within our community giving back. In 1921 Mrs. Louis M. Forsythe Demarest, whose daughter loved Mendham, made a bequest in her will, leaving a lot on Hilltop Road and funds to construct a library building. In June 1922 the building was dedicated in memory of her daughter, Sarah Forsythe Demarest.

In addition to the land and money for the construction of the building, the Demarest Will provided an endowment to be used for the support of the library. The fund served the needs of the library until 1956, when a formal petition was made to the borough council requesting $3,000 for support of the library. The council appropriated $1,000 and continued to do so for several years, increasing the amount annually to $4,000 in 1975 and now to more than $150,000.

From 1960 on, Mendham was to have a period of change and growth. In time, the county and the state would become more involved in the operation of libraries. In late 1964 the Morris County librarian proposed that the Mendham Borough and Mendham Township libraries merge. This set off meetings, surveys, and proposals, and the League of Women Voters prepared an extensive study. It appeared at first blush that this was a viable option, but by the late 1970s the merger idea died.

In 1976 Andrew Fletcher, a member of the library board since 1954 and president from 1960 to 1973, made a generous gift of $75,000 that allowed the library to double its size with a two-story wing, and another $75,000 upon completion for its maintenance—enough of an endowment to continue operations. Upon his death in 1977, the library board received an additional $50,000. The Andrew Fletcher Wing was dedicated in 1978.

We have come a long way from the first lending library of primarily religious books to today's high-tech minifacility in its neatly designed, charming, and compact 1920s brick building at 10 Hilltop Road. The library boasts six computers for patrons' use, along with a high-speed copying machine. When the circulation staff checks out materials, it is done via computer. The collection of materials for patron enjoyment is composed of approximately 40,000 books, 650 audio books, 100 periodicals, 500 DVDs, and 200 VHS videos. Can you image the first settlers trying to grapple with something called a DVD?

Reflecting on the library contents, we are reminded that Kate Emmons, Ella Mockridge, and other local historians began the current collection of materials, artifacts, and photos in our library historical archives more than thirty years ago. Their efforts, in addition to those of many others, allow us to continue to understand our history and our community.

Left: Andrew Fletcher, mayor, library and borough benefactor. *Mendham Borough archives*

Right: Borough library dedication. *Mendham Borough Library archives*

Chapter Two: When Grass Grew on Main Street

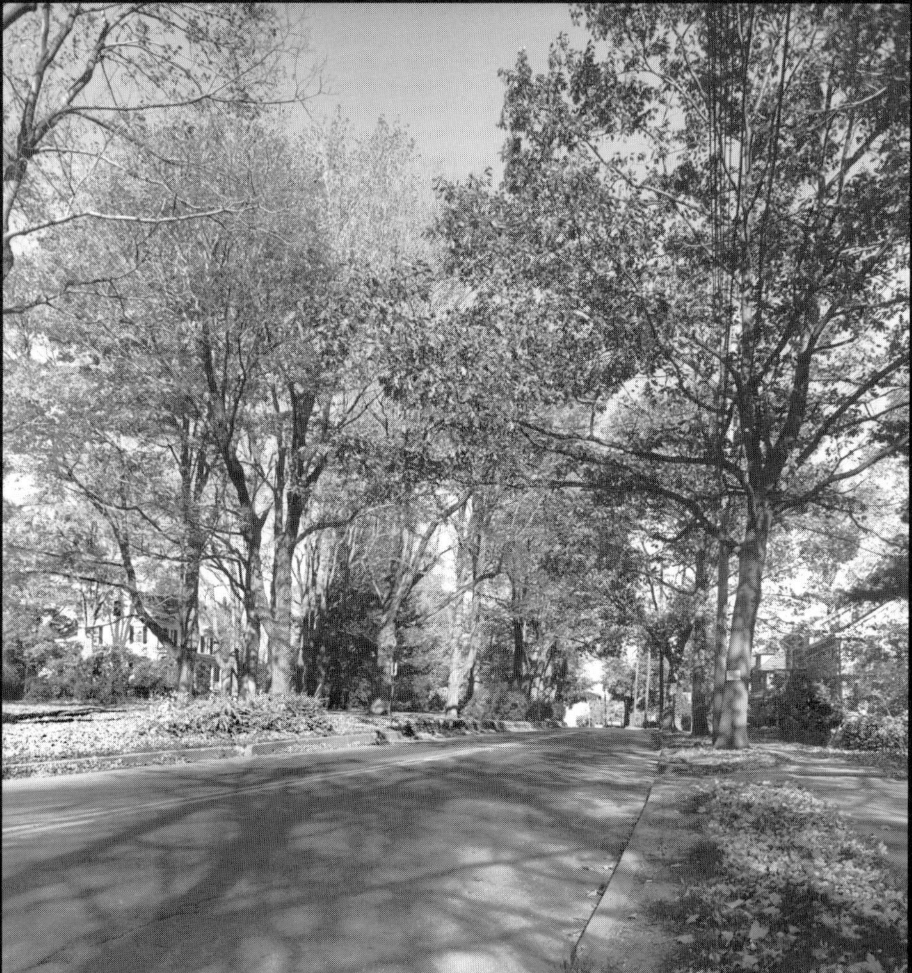

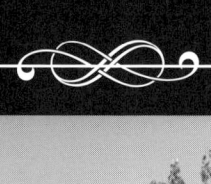

Chapter Three
A Walk through Our Neighborhoods

Without community pride and civic pride that prevailed among our fellow townsmen, all our accomplishments would have been lost. It all cost time, money and effort, but it was all worthwhile.

—Mayor Bowers, December 1950

While the Historic District of Mendham Borough is central to its village character, the surrounding homesteads, farms, and estates that existed in the 1800 and 1900s set the stage for the neighborhoods and streetscapes in today's borough. Through the years, the names of our streets and subdivisions have remembered people in our history, the land they have owned, and the varying ways they have contributed to the community and society through service or leadership. Names such as Garabrant, Lowery, Talmage, Bliss, Cromwell, Gunther, Pitney, Franklin, Hoffman, and Bockoven are familiar to many of us. While the once open land of Mendham Borough has been sold and subdivided over the years, many of the original owners have not been forgotten. Established "Mendhamites" still refer to land by the name of the owner they remember.

Let's borrow a fine carriage from the Freemans, a horse from the Black Horse Stables, or a new motorbus from George Gunther at the Mendham Garage. Forget about time periods, and let's visit our neighborhoods as they might have been at some time during the last one hundred years. Visit the diverse group of people from varying backgrounds and timeframes that have formed our community.

Dr. F. Clyde Bowers joins Peggy and Ike Cramer, longtime residents of Park Avenue, in a 1952 ride at Borough Park. *Courtesy of Margaret Cramer*

North to Mendham Mountain

Traveling north on Mountain, we wave a hello to Mr. Robinson at the drugstore and the butcher, barber, and shoemaker as they open their small shops for the day. Moving past today's Borough Park and Gazebo, we recall that the telephone and fire alarm center was once located on this corner. The home where it resided was moved to make way for the park.

Florie Farms

As we step back in time, we see one of Mr. Pietro Clementi's cows loose on Mountain Avenue. It has come from the area that today is lined with homes along Florie Farm Road, Phoenix, Hoffman, Bowers, and Knollwood Drives. Close your eyes and visualize a dairy farm that extended east from Mountain Avenue just above Garabrant Street down Dean Road to Knollwood and north from Dean to Mountain Valley Park. Coming to Mendham as a twenty-four-year-old, well liked and respected Sicilian immigrant Pietro "Pete"

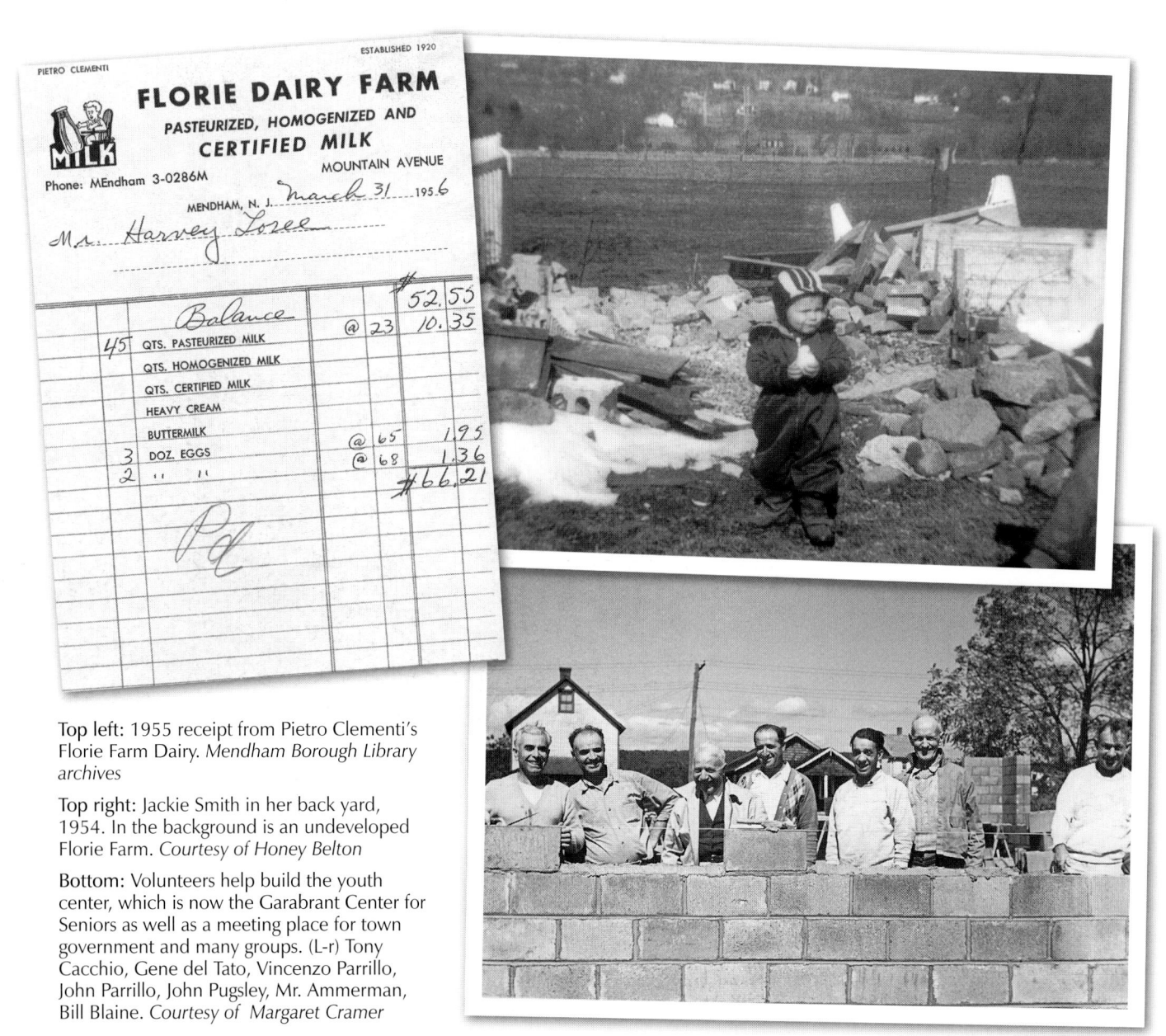

Top left: 1955 receipt from Pietro Clementi's Florie Farm Dairy. *Mendham Borough Library archives*

Top right: Jackie Smith in her back yard, 1954. In the background is an undeveloped Florie Farm. *Courtesy of Honey Belton*

Bottom: Volunteers help build the youth center, which is now the Garabrant Center for Seniors as well as a meeting place for town government and many groups. (L-r) Tony Cacchio, Gene del Tato, Vincenzo Parrillo, John Parrillo, John Pugsley, Mr. Ammerman, Bill Blaine. *Courtesy of Margaret Cramer*

Clementi developed the dairy farm named for his wife, Florence (Taylor), and owned the land from 1920 until it was sold for subdivision as Florie Farm Estates in the 1960s.

Recognizable in his short-sleeved, plaid flannel shirt even in winter, he delivered bottled milk fresh each day to Mendham doorsteps. While his barn, farmhouse, and cows are gone now, we remember him through the wonderful gift of land encompassing the Mountain Valley Pool, built in 1945 for the children of Mendham. Rumor has it that the quid pro quo for the gift was that no longer was anyone allowed to complain about Mr. Clementi's wandering cows. Perhaps Mr. Clementi also wanted the children to stop shooing away his cows from the watering hole near Knollwood so they could use his pond for swimming.

As we open our eyes, we see Mountain Valley Pool referred to as the "mud hole" by some locals. It was built on the site referred to as "Hoffman Pond," named after the landowner before Pietro Clement, John F. Hoffman. The days of swimming at the "mud hole" are gone, but we still enjoy fishing and ice skating, and recently a new bridge was installed. We can still see the remains of the beach and can imagine the lifeguard chairs. We cannot miss a stone monument at the site honoring Mr. Clementi as the donor of the land.

In addition to the Phoenix family, proprietors of the Phoenix House, John F. Hoffman and Dr. Clyde Bowers are remembered in the street names of Florie Farm Estates.

Mendham's Mountain Valley Pool, unfortunately referred to as "the mud hole," is enjoyed thanks to Pietro Clementi and the volunteers who built it. Photo by John Andrus

- **Dr. F. Clyde Bowers** *was a well-known physician and chief of staff at Morristown Memorial Hospital who also served as mayor of the borough from 1947 to 1950. He was labeled a "country doctor" who was known to accept payment in produce when funds were not available, answer phones,*

Phil and Cora Parrillo tour Mountain Avenue by sled in 1944. *Courtesy of Honey Belton*

View from center of town north on Mountain Avenue before the roads were paved. *Courtesy of Don Preziosi*

Looking east from Mountain at the Mendham Rock-a-bye Station. *Courtesy of Don Preziosi*

Left: The Smiths enjoy the Mountain Valley Pool in the 1950s. *Courtesy of Honey Belton*

Right: The very beginning of what would eventually be named the Mountain Valley Pool. *Courtesy of Honey Belton*

and maintain flexible hours. During WWII he served as the only doctor in the Mendham and Chester area. As a doctor and a mayor, he was instrumental in helping to bring the pasteurization of milk to the area. The borough's Bowers Building is also named in honor of our "country doctor."

- *John F. Hoffman was a local builder, councilman from 1906 to 1913, and the borough's first fire chief. Among some of the most remembered buildings he constructed are Franklin Farms, St. John Baptist Convent, Bernardsville Public School, and the Bernardsville Railroad Station. He was a previous owner of some of the Florie Farm land.*

Rock-a-bye Baby

Adjacent to the pond, one sees Patriot's Path and can remember that the park path follows the route of the Rockaway Valley Railway. Established here in 1891, it was more appropriately called the Rock-a-bye Railroad, owing to its bumpy ride. It was here on Mountain Avenue that the Mendham station existed and that Michael Coghlan put the Mendham mail on the train to Morristown. That must have been a relief to him, as his twice-daily trip to Morristown by horse and carriage was no longer necessary.

The Rockaway Valley Railroad (RVRR), the only railroad that ever came through the Mendhams, lasted just twenty-two years. Had we visited in 1913, we would have seen the last train pass. The railroad played an important role following the incorporation of the borough, as pipes and supplies needed for the water distribution system arrived via its delivery. Calvin Davis, who kept a historical journal for the Mendhams, wrote: "For its facilities in freight and express service the railroad was of inestimable benefit to Mendham. Lumber, coal, and heavy construction materials as well as commercial merchandise

---

How did the Mendham swimming hole get its name?

Answer: Honey Parrillo Belton named it "Mountain Valley Pool" in a contest. She won a $25 war bond.

Chapter Three: A Walk through Our Neighborhoods

Residents gather for the annual Garabrant Block Party. *Courtesy of Chris McManus*

Under control at the Garabrant Party, organized by the McManuses. *Courtesy of Chris McManus*

Neighbors gather at the Einhorns. *Courtesy of Ginny Beutnagel*

were carried in considerable quantities, and for a number of years its operation was a promising impetus to the commercial and industrial growth of Mendham."

In September 1906 the borough's budget was increased $700 to match an equal amount of state aid for building Mountain Avenue from the village center to the Mendham railroad station. The role that leaders and founders of the borough played in the history of the RVRR is significant. The cover of *Images of America, The Mendhams* by John W. Rae pictures the railroad's founders as passengers on the first run from Mendham on June 17, 1891. Other passengers included James K. Burd, Marius B. Robinson, T. W. Phoenix, John D. Lindsey, and Robert Ararat of Mendham. Burd and Lindsey were present for the borough's first meeting of incorporation.

The RVRR started with a four-and-a-half-mile section from Whitehouse to Oldwick in March 1888 for the purposes of hauling peaches. Another section to Potterville was added during the second year, and then a year later to Gladstone. The line's longest trestle was constructed, and the track was extended to Mendham in 1891, ending in Watnong near Morristown on July 30, 1892. When completed, RVRR covered some twenty-five miles.

The railroad acquired its nickname as a function of its construction and ride. Light rails were spiked to squared-off logs with a long gap (spaced twice that of a normal track) between each railroad tie. Although the railroad followed the normal practice for laying tracks to follow a stream, which provided a more level route, it was noted for its up-and-down ride. As the country dipped and rolled, so did the track, keeping the passengers rocking and rolling on the "Rock-a-bye Baby."

1952 flag raising at Morris Savings Bank, site of the Great Bank Robbery. The structure is now the Bowers Building. (L-r) Harold Patterson, Gloria Patterson Lawrence, Ralph Welsh; (far right) Cindy Burke. In background are Jean and Harold Patterson Sr. *Courtesy of Cindy Burke*

Chapter Three: A Walk through Our Neighborhoods

In 1895 the San Jose scale killed the local peach trees. As a result, the RVRR suffered significant loss in revenue. Although the railroad continued hauling freight and passengers, it was not very profitable. The Public Utility Commission of New Jersey in 1910 imposed requirements for upgrading the railroad that were too costly for the owners to implement, and after a long, hard struggle, the company died a financial death. Train service ended October 13, 1913, following a January 24 fire that destroyed the Watnong Depot. Some wealthy estate owners did not bemoan the end of the Rock-a-bye Baby, believing that it attracted unwanted hobos. In July 1917 fifteen hundred tons of rails were removed and shipped to France for scrap iron for Allied armaments. Today the old right-of-way is Patriot's Path.

Reminiscing

Before turning around and heading back up Mountain Avenue, we can look up to the mountains and off to the west, past Mountainside toward Combs Hollow Road. That's where we would have found Mendham Borough's first reservoir. It's also close to the location of a "Jersey Lightning" still explosion well remembered by longtime residents. The reservoir is dry now; however, the story of its development and the role of water in our history will always exist. It was also from the top of this hill that our local children would sleigh-ride down Calais and Mountain.

As our horses move up the dirt road toward town, we pass Maple Avenue to the west. Beyond the homes to the rear are fields that were undoubtedly part of the Bockoven Farm that stretched for many acres from Cosma Place to Mountain Avenue and between Maple Avenue and Garabrant Street as well as off West Main Street. We may catch a glimpse of children riding horses in

Today's Patriot's Path has replaced the tracks of the only railroad ever to have come through Mendham.

Corner of Mountain and Mountainside during a dusty summer, ca. 1908. *Courtesy of Don Preziosi*

the field or cutting down the hay to play a game of baseball. While there are many older homes in that area, the "new" development didn't come in until the land was subdivided in the late 1960s. Later, we will be visiting the main farmhouse of the Bockovens on Main Street.

Passing Garabrant Street, we remember the many Garabrants who lived in various areas in town and contributed in different ways to our community. The Garabrant Center, originally the borough youth center and now our Senior Citizens Center and meeting place, carries the name of the family.

- *J. W. Garabrant came to Mendham in 1871 and was known for operating the stagecoach to Morristown in which he carried the mail; running the butcher shop; serving as postmaster for eight years; and operating an ice business from New Street for twenty-five years before the invention of the electric refrigerator. He served in government as the borough tax collector and treasurer from 1906 to 1921 and was clerk of the school board.*

- *Everett L. Garabrant was a contractor, builder, and president of Mendham's bus company. When his horse-drawn bus ended service in Mendham in 1929, he joined with John M. Hoffman and Lewis Hill to form the Mendham Garage Company, which offered transportation via a large, open passenger truck with a capacity to accommodate twenty passengers. The motor service continued with the same fare policy: 40 cents one way and 75 cents round trip to Morristown.*

Heading back to the center of town, we waive at the Cillos and the Pennimpedes, longtime residents of the town, who remember it when . . . .

An old-time sledder's view looking south halfway down Mountainside from the Calais Corner. *Courtesy of Ernie Maw*

Chapter Three: A Walk through Our Neighborhoods

West to Roxiticus

Riding west on Main Street, we wave to the butcher, pass the Freeman horseshoe shop, and bid good morning to the people-watchers on the upstairs porch of the firehouse.

Hoffman's

Located in today's yellow Weickert Building, the first firehouse was built in 1906 and nicknamed "Hoffman Hall." The building, constructed by Mr. Hoffman, a general contractor, was located next to his home, where he provided a shed to house the borough's first fire truck until the firehouse was completed. Use your imagination, and you still may hear music coming from the third floor of "Hoffman Hall," where dances, opera, and shows were held.

In a small alley in the area, you can also imagine "Little It-ly," as it was referred to by the older Mendhamites. When John Hoffman wanted to work on the construction of estates at the turn of the twentieth century, he realized that the masonry skill did not exist in "wooden-built" Mendham. At that time, Italian masons were the most skilled, so he recruited them. Hoffman brought about a half-dozen Italian masons and their families to Mendham, building simple frame houses for them behind his own, on the site of the nineteenth-century tannery. The immigrant masons remained there until they were able to build or buy their own homes. The homes are now gone.

Residents Remembered

Also in the area and located on the southern side of West Main Street is the Babbitt School, which operated from 1881 to 1901. The original part of the school became the kitchen wing of the home built on the lot.

Continuing the journey away from the center of town, we see several residences, some dating back to Colonial times. We pass the Old Methodist Parsonage and the Thompson Home, individually listed on the National Register of Historic Places. Captain David Thompson was a Revolutionary War officer who organized the Mendham Company of the minutemen in 1775. During the winter of 1779, when General George Washington's Army was camped at Jockey Hollow, Thompson and his wife opened their home to soldiers needing food and shelter.

To the north is the Cosma Lake section of town. Previously composed of summer cottages, where oil lamps provided illumination and buried fifty-five-gallon drums provided septic, it was an area for summer fun. Jack and Sophie Swatsworth can still recall the "Newarkers" who would buy blocks of ice at

Top: The rebuilt Bockoven Farmhouse. The Bockovens owned huge tracts of farmland west of the borough center. *Mendham Borough archives*

Bottom: Looking west when grass really did grow on Main Street, ca. 1903. *Mendham Borough archives*

Deerfield Diners Dinner Group, begun in 1999 by Linda and Marshall Sussman, encourages neighbors to get to know one another. Seldom do you walk or drive through Deerfield without getting a friendly wave. (L-r) Tim Ide, Jean Ide, Heather St. John, Joan Debuvitz, Bill Debuvutz. *Courtesy of Linda Sussman*

Deerfield residents participate in lighting of the luminaria on Christmas Eve. The tradition was started by Bev and Andy Emory in 1989, and there has been 100 percent participation for years. *Courtesy of Linda Sussman*

Deerfield social activity. (L-r) Marshall Sussman, Dave Sprandel, Cathy McGrath, Bette Sprandel, Mike McGrath, Lesly Straub, Cliff Straub. *Courtesy of Linda Sussman*

Above: Aerial view of Deerfield prior to its development. *Mendham Borough archives*

Left: The bell tower at St. John Baptist, although well to the west of the Borough Center, can been seen above the tree line from the Borough Park. *Photo by John Andrus*

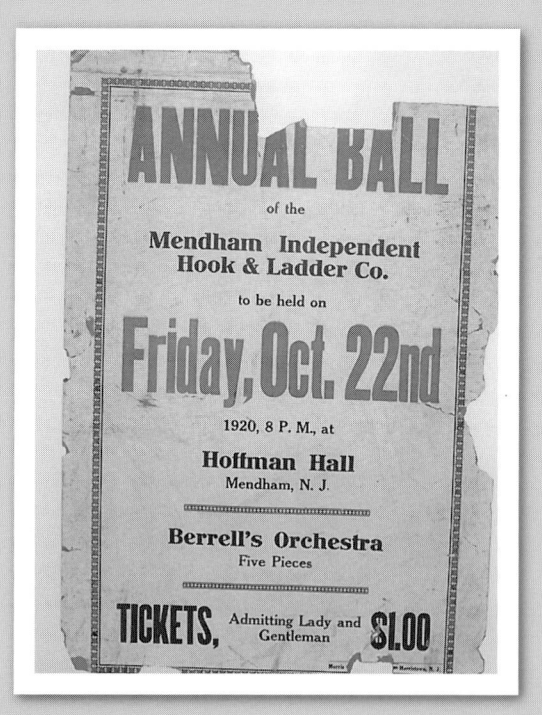

Above: In 1920, residents could support the fire department by dancing to an orchestra at Hoffman Hall. *Courtesy of Mendham Fire Department*

Top left: The original firehouse, completed in 1906, is today known as the yellow Weichert building. *Courtesy of Ernie Maw*

Bottom left: Reflections of the past—the David Thompson home on West Main Street. *Courtesy of Ernie Maw*

Left: Aerial view of St. John Baptist. *Courtesy of Don Preziosi*

Right: St. John Baptist school bus. *Courtesy of Ella Mockridge, "Our Mendham"*

the depot in Morristown, strap them to the running boards of their cars, and enjoy barrels of beer in the Cosma bungalows. Most nights, they were content to sleep on the floors. It is doubtful they would recognize the expanded and improved homes now.

As we reach the open farmlands ahead, we stop for homemade pies at Keppler's Stand on the corner of Main Street and Lake Drive. Across the street, we can hear the children playing soccer on West Field, land donated by the DeNeufville family.

Before reaching Roxiticus Hill, one can see St. Hilda's Lodge to the south, built by William Cordingley for the Sisters of St. John Baptist around 1920. Cordingley, an architect, also designed St. John Baptist School and several homes in this area. He served as borough councilman and mayor. Through the years, Cordingley was involved in many controversial borough issues, and he also helped out many townspeople by making anonymous donations of coal to those who could not afford it.

Bockoven Farms

Heading back toward town, we look to the north and visualize fields that encompass the area off Country Lane and North Linden Lanes. These are the Bockoven fields, which extended from Maple and Mountain Avenue. The original farmhouse located on West Main Street was moved across the fields to the northwest to its location on Farmhouse Lane. The original home has been demolished; however, one with a strong resemblance still appears. A portion of the Bockoven property was subdivided to form the neighborhood today, that consists of North Linden Lane, Deerfield Road, and Loryn and Glenbrook Lanes. Another portion of the property was part of the Country Acres subdivision incorporating Country Lane, Bockoven Road, Gunther Street, and parts of Maple Avenue.

As we get back toward town, let's just make a quick stop at the apple orchard at the corner of New and Prospect Streets. If they're not too busy getting a shipment of apples ready to be sent to the distillery, perhaps we can get a free sample . . . of the apples, that is.

East—The Road to Morristown

Our next trip takes us on the road to Morristown. Leaving town, we pass the first location of the post office, on the northeast corner of West Main and Hilltop, and the plumbing and hardware store that today is St. Mark's Parish House.

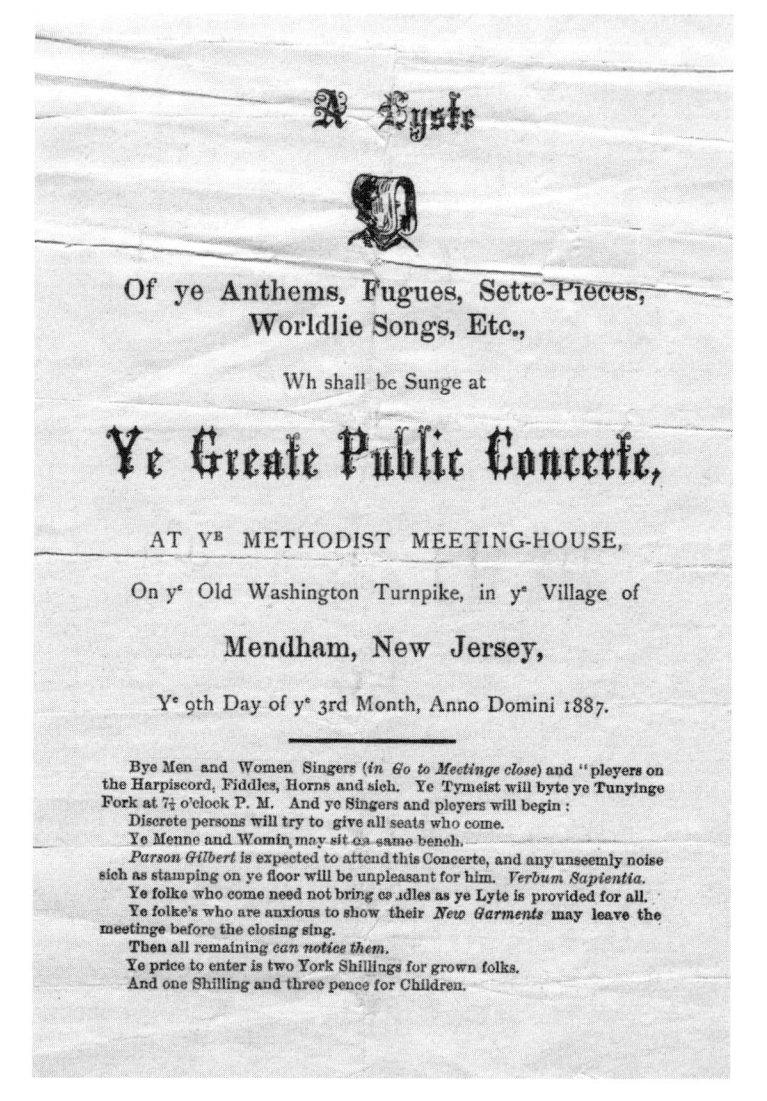

Top left: A postcard from Bedford, Iowa, notified the borough fire department that its firehouse made *Ripley's Believe It or Not* for its many uses. *Courtesy of Mendham Fire Department*

Bottom left: In the 1890s the Methodist church served as the opera house. *Mendham Borough Library archives*

Right: In 1887 a public concert was held at the Methodist Meetinghouse. Behave . . . Parson Gilbert will be in attendance. *Mendham Borough archives*

Ripley's Believe It or Not

To the left, where the firehouse entrance is now located, we see the town hall, and we know that this building was moved back and incorporated into the current firehouse that was built in 1980. Who knew that the Borough of Mendham would appear in *Ripley's Believe It or Not* because of the building's many uses? Originally constructed as the Methodist Church and located closer to the center of town, it was then moved down West Main Street when the new church was constructed. Before it was integrated with today's firehouse, it served as the Mendham Township Town Hall, the Mendham Borough Town Hall and Firehouse, and the Mendham Opera House. According to Kate Emmons, some of the town minstrel shows were held there. In 1906 the rental fee for a performance of three nights was $15. In

In the early 1930s, the building that is Sorrento's Pizza was a luncheonette. It later became known as the Mendham Tea Room. *Courtesy of Don Preziosi*

The Cole House at 34 East Main Street. *Courtesy of Ernie Maw*

On July 7, 1977, the best show in town was watching the Freeman Ayers' "new" house move from the site of the new post office to 50 Main Street. After obtaining permission from the government, Mr. Freeman saved the Ayers home from demolition. *Mendham Borough Library archives*

Photo of Lou Moro at Moro's Automotive was included in the time capsule buried in 1976.

61

Top left: The firehouse in the mid-1900s. *Mendham Borough Library archives*

Top right: Top half of the church moves to become the top part of the 1980s firehouse. *Courtesy of Carolyn Menagh*

Bottom: Parks Plumbing stood where the Peapack–Gladstone Bank stands. Before it was a bank, the site was a multifamily housing unit. *Mendham Borough Library archives*

fact, a 1913 Sanborne map of Mendham also shows an entry for "movies." If we look at today's firehouse from the east side, we can see the round front window of the original building.

Wheelrights to Chevrolet Dealers

The next left is Orchard Street, which was called Gunther Avenue, according to an old tax map. Why? The area from Main Street on either side of Orchard to the end of the road where Mountain View School is currently situated belonged, in large part, to the Gunther family. For many years, the Gunthers had a variety of businesses at the corner of Gunther and Main, where the Audi dealership stands today.

John Henry Gunther came to Mendham in 1853. He was a cabinetmaker and wheelright, and in 1860 he established a carriage house and carpenter shop on the site that became Gunther Motors around 1916. His son, Jacob Smith Gunther, was born in Mendham in 1862, and after learning the trade, he purchased the business from his father and set up shop repairing and painting all kinds of wagons and buggies. In 1912 he and his brother, George Gunther, opened the garage that stood at the corner of Orchard and Main

Street for many years. Eventually, George Gunther left the garage business and started a taxi business. Gunther's Garage became the agent for Will Overland, and in 1916 they had the first association with the Chevrolet Motor Company. They sold their first automobile for $580.

J. Smith Gunther's two sons, Walter and James Hall, also had their start in the old carriage shop. In 1924 they decided to go into the automotive business and in 1926 incorporated as Gunther Motors Inc. They became a direct dealer for Chevrolet automobiles. The old buildings were not torn down until 1930—seventy-five years after John Henry Gunther built them. Then a new building was built, only to be destroyed by fire on June 12, 1996. The Audi dealership was then constructed on the site. While Gunther Avenue has since been renamed Orchard Street to appropriately reflect the orchard that stood by the borough park, to many, the corner will always be associated with the family.

Top left: Gunther Motors in 1925. A fire on June 12, 1996 (black billowing smoke was seen for miles) destroyed the building. It is now an Audi dealership. *Courtesy of Ernie Maw*

Top right: The Gunther Wagon Shop about 1927. It stood west of Gunther Motors. *Courtesy of Ernie Maw*

Bottom left: Pre-1905, the Methodist Church was the township hall. *Mendham Borough Library archives*

Bottom right: The old Methodist church was, at various times, Mendham Supply Company and a lumber, millwork, and hardware store. *Mendham Borough Library*

Chapter Three: A Walk through Our Neighborhoods

Hilltop Dairy Farm

Cows again . . . this time grazing at the high school, which is built on land where a prosperous dairy farm and hayfield once stood. Since the 1800s, the land on which West Morris Mendham High School stands has had only a few owners.

Surprisingly, in the twenty-first century we still see sheep grazing on a field east of the high school and Grace Lutheran Church. The "sheep farm," about eight acres and now belonging to the Rowe family, provides a well known and important streetscape and ambiance that reminds us of Mendham's open space and farming days. Thanks to the Rowe family, every effort has been made to retain this piece of Mendham history as preserved farmland.

A local story about the red barn that stands on the property relates that during WWI, the "Hilltop farm" painted on the top of the roof was covered over to remove any pertinent landmarks for enemy planes. The area is also known for the little red house, the "Lillie House," which stands next to it. That home was built around 1830 and was the first one built on a tract of land owned by Ebenezer Byram.

Standing on the original tract of land is the Grace Lutheran Church. The Board of Missions of the American Lutheran Church purchased the property in January 1966. If we stop and reflect a moment, we can see the first group of prospective members meeting in February 1967 for a progressive dinner as they made plans for their church. The initial *Channels of Grace Church* was printed, and other firsts quickly followed: the youth group met, the first choir rehearsed, and despite a late winter storm, the first service of public worship was held at the Brookside Community Club in March 1967. Again we can see the people of the area coming together to work on this new church, building chancel furniture, painting walls, designing and sewing robes, vestments, paraments and stoles, cleaning the building, and installing the landscaping. May 28, 1967, was established as Grace's "birthday." Groundbreaking for a new addition was held in October 1990, beginning a new decade of growth.

Top: Rowe's Sheep Farm still has a welcome and distinctive impact on the borough's landscape. *Photo by John Andrus*

Bottom: Grace Lutheran Church, 2006.

Lambertville (N. J.) Record, November 20, 1913.

MENDHAM COUPLE CELEBRATE GOLDEN WEDDING ANNIVERSARY

Mr. and Mrs. William Menagh Wedded Fifty Years Ago in Morris County Town Where Lambertville Record is Widely Read.

MENDHAM, N. J., NOV. 19 — (Special Correspondent of Lambertville Record and Coryell Courier)—Mr. and Mrs. William Menagh celebrated the fiftieth anniversary of their marriage at their home in this borough yesterday. Sixty-four persons were present, including three who were in attendance fifty years ago—Mrs. Menagh's sister, Mrs. Angeline Robinson, of Newark; Mahlon Cole, a brother, of Morristown; and Mrs. M. M. Henry, a cousin, from Riverside, California.

Mrs. Menagh, who was Miss Julia Ann Cole, was born at Hacklebarney, and Mr. Menagh was born at Beattyestown. They were married at Mendham on November 18, 1863, by Rev. David Magee, D. D., pastor of the First Presbyterian Church. They resided on their farm near this borough for many years, before moving into town. Later Mr. Menagh sold the farm to former-Governor Franklin Murphy.

The children—Mrs. William Osmun, of Newark; George Menagh, of Irvington, and James Menagh, of Mendham—gave fifty white roses, and the "bride and groom" also received fifty dollars in gold, besides many other beautiful gifts. Luncheon was served from 3 to 5 o'clock.

Mr. Menagh is 76 years of age, and Mrs. Menagh 75. Besides the three children named above, they have eight grandchildren—Misses Helen, Julia, Bessie, Alice, Ruth and Emily and William Menagh, of Mendham, and Ralph Osmun, of Newark.

The Stagecoach Stop

Stepping back in time and looking to our eastern border, we see an oak tree standing at the triangle at the intersection of Cold Hill Road and Main Street. The corner that today bears the "Welcome to Mendham Borough" sign is a gateway to our community. At one time a stopping point for the stagecoach, the Triangle has long been voluntarily maintained by the Mendham Garden Club.

Franklin Farms

If we look to the right, in the distance we can see a large country home built by Aaron Hudson on property that was later known as Franklin Farms. While the main house of the property is located east of Cold Hill Road on Route 24 in Mendham Township, the original Franklin Farm Estate extended into Mendham Borough. The homes on Franklin, Ogden, Drake, Leddell, Babbitt, and Budd are part of the Franklin Farms Estates subdivision.

When the builder finished this home, the perspective buyer could not afford it, and it was then purchased by Francis Oliver, who for many years ran it as a boardinghouse known as Oliver Hall. In 1909 Franklin Murphy, New Jersey's thirty-fifth governor, gave the farm his name as he accumulated four hundred acres for his estate.

Left: 1913 golden anniversary announcement of Mr. and Mrs. William Menagh references the sale of property to former New Jersey Governor Murphy. Although Franklin Farms, the governor's mansion, is located in the township, the farmland extended into today's area of the same name. *Courtesy of William Menagh Sr.*

Top right: The garden club decorates a Christmas tree at the Triangle in 1969 before its award-winning renovation project. *Courtesy of Mendham Garden Club*

Bottom right: Stagecoach stop at the Oak Tree Triangle area in the 1800s. *Courtesy of Don Preziosi*

Chapter Three: A Walk through Our Neighborhoods

We know we have been visualizing, but Africa . . . zebras . . . llamas . . . rare birds? Yes, in 1926 the Franklin Farms Estate was purchased by a collector of rare birds and animals, including llamas and a zebra. In fact, we have heard that Dr. De Groot, who had his veterinary clinic on East Main Street, was the vet for the Franklin Farms Estate and cared for these animals. In 1942 the estate was purchased again and eventually subdivided. The home was also used as a private school. Today the remaining property around the home is being subdivided in the township for new homes.

The street names of the Franklin Farms Estates subdivision appropriately allow us to recall people who made a mark on the history of Mendham.

- *Franklin:* New Jersey's fifth governor; owner of the estate in 1909.
- *Drake:* Early settlers to Mendham; original home located in Drake's Clearing on the western side of Cold Hill Road; assisted during the Revolutionary War by housing sick soldiers.
- *Leddell:* Several members of the family practiced medicine in the Mendham area beginning in the 1700s; owned sawmills and gristmills in the Jockey Hollow area.
- *Babbitt:* Misses Babbitt established a private school in Mendham in 1861. In the 1700s, a Mr. Babbitt was known to sled to Morristown with Mendham supplies for the Revolutionary soldiers.
- *Dayton:* The Daytons were settled in Mendham in the 1700s. Some of the Mendham Daytons moved to Ohio in the late 1800s, and Dayton, Ohio, was named.

Top left: Caroling at the Mendham Commons, 1982. *Courtesy of Carol Houston*

Top right: MASH senior citizen housing.

Bottom: Mendham Commons Block Party, 2003. *Courtesy of Carol Houston*

2006 East Main streetscape, part of the historic district. The borough is attempting to retain its historic look.
Photo by Michael Gaffney

Frank and Helen Martino, half-century-plus residents, celebrate their fiftieth wedding anniversary as Frank Jr. presides.
Photo by John Andrus

Drake's Clearing

Looking north to Drake's Clearing and the family homestead, we see another one of our more modern-day neighborhoods, the Commons. Mendham Commons is a three hundred-unit townhouse community located at the northeast corner of the borough. It is built on land formerly owned by the Drake family, one of the earliest settlers of Mendham, and is nestled between the hills of what is now Mendham Township and a tributary of the North Branch of the Raritan River.

The townhouse complex is spread over 120 acres of woods, lawn, and hundreds of mature trees and shrubs. The two-and-a-half-acre pond that was created to capture the muddy water runoff from the initial construction is now a lovely oasis located on the southern boundary of the property beyond the swimming pool and a small meadow. Although this was a controversial planned-unit development when it was brought before the Borough Council and Planning Board in 1969, many longtime Mendham residents now call the Commons home.

The Hillcrest Avenue Touch Football Game has been played every Thanksgiving morning for twenty-one years. The pre-turkey workout, suggested by Bob Everts (front left) is gender-neutral and has included players from five to sixty-three years of age. (Some mothers believe their sons fly home just to see them.)

The Sisters of Christian Charity celebrate seventy-five years in Mendham Borough. *Courtesy of Sisters of Christian Charity*

Left: Stopping for a drink at the corner of Bernardsville Road and Pleasant Valley Road, 1800s. *Courtesy of Don Preziosi*

Right: The road to Bernardsville around 1800. *Courtesy of Don Preziosi*

Continuing toward the center of town, it's impossible to miss the Mendham Village Shopping Center. Quite different from yesterday's shops, many enterprises remain in the control of local residents who can enjoy a short commute as well as the opportunity to barter with friends and neighbors. While we have only Kings Supermarket today, Jack Turpin recalls the fifties, when there were four grocery stores in the center of town. Fagan's store has evolved into Mendham Liquors—but it's still a Fagan store. And Mendham Hardware has now changed hands and location, but Dot Kuepferle can still find much of the merchandise sold for many years by the family hardware store.

Have you ever wondered what lies at the end of the private drive just west of Mendham Village Shopping Center? Since 1980, Mendham Area Senior Housing (MASH) has been providing independent, federally funded housing for seniors and the disabled. They celebrated their twenty-fifth anniversary in 2005. Today there are forty-two residents living on the 7.8 acres originally owned by Jake Lewis. The MASH community room not only hosts events for the residents, but is utilized for local blood drives, church-sponsored dinners, and voting for Mendham's 5th District.

In addition to providing housing, MASH coordinates the Mendham Area Senior Transportation service for our community. This service, affectionately called the "MASH Mobile," is supported by funds from both Mendham Borough and Mendham Township. Transportation is provided for all Mendham senior citizens over the age of sixty and disabled adults over the age of eighteen. This service enables many of our homebound neighbors to enjoy more active and independent lives by being able to manage medical and social appointments themselves.

The Mendham Interchurch group originally conceived the idea for MASH and worked with the borough to make the idea a reality. As we pass by, we note that life at MASH can be as active or as quiet as the tenant wishes. Local community and church groups provide extra activities and services to the tenants; these include senior lunches, dinners, craft days, monthly birthday celebrations, game days, occasion-related transportation, bingo, student and Scout visitations, Bible studies, fellowship hour, Christmas caroling, gift certificates, Meals on Wheels, group exercise, and movies.

> *What did Jake Lewis do to prevent teenagers from regularly stealing a large stone sign from his front lawn on East Main Street?*
>
> *Answer: Slathered it with Vaseline*

Chapter Three: A Walk through Our Neighborhoods

The stone watering trough remains today, but the mode of transport has changed.
Photo by Michael Gaffney

South—The Road to Bernardsville

The southern area of Mendham Borough began its development in the late 1800s and early 1900s, when many summer homes and estates were built by financiers and industrialists from the New York area. Given the prominence of Morristown—which became known as the "millionaire city," it is no surprise that many vacationers would be introduced to the area for a summer stay. The railroad was extended from New York to Bernardsville, and the Somerset Inn in Bernardsville was established. As more land in the area around Morristown was purchased, socialites from New York began to build in the area known as Mine Mountain and Millionaire's Mountain—to us, the Bernardsville Mountain. In Mendham Borough these included such names as Talmage, Bliss, and Cromwell. Not surprisingly, these names are remembered in today's street names. These socialites led the borough's ride into the Gilded Age!

Before we reach the estates, we bear right and pass Mendham's last cider mill and distillery, located off Hilltop Road. The mill was built against the hill on three levels. The horse-drawn wagons ascended and backed up against a door to the mill's top floor, where the apples were received.

There is some traffic in this part of town—apple wagons are going to the distillery, and construction wagons heading from the Rock-a-bye will be going this way with building supplies for the mansions. Also, villagers are passing by on their way to work at the mansions. If we are lucky, we might also see some estate residents, known as "cottagers," driving their carriages pulled by four horses. Messrs. Talmage, Bliss, and Cromwell are known to have driven these carriages, known as "four in hands."

Cromwell Estate

While we pass through the next portion of Hilltop Road and see new homes on the hilltops, we are reminded that in the early 1900s, the Sandrellin Estate,

A Legend

One of the legends surrounding the Sisters of Christian Charity's early history is how they acquired their property. A member of the present motherhouse shares this treasured memory of her novitiate days:

"More than a century ago, I recall, Sister Raphaele Klein, then superior at St. Michael's Elizabeth, shared with two first-year novices from Elizabeth an intimate experience which she treasured in her own heart.

Sister Raphaele related that she had been assigned by the major superiors to find a forty-acre tract on which to establish a new motherhouse for the proposed Eastern Province. A good-natured parishioner from St. Michael's was asked to chauffeur her and a companion around the North Jersey area to find land for sale. They made many trips—all to no avail. One final look—and it all seemed so futile!

Suddenly, a man seated on a white horse approached them and asked if he could be of help.

They told him of their vain searching and their many disappointments. He thought a minute and suggested they ride a little father along the road. There was a piece of property for sale a short distance up the road. Though it was larger than forty acres, perhaps it would do! And the man on the white horse disappeared in front of their very eyes before they could thank him. Sister Raphaele claimed it was good St. Joseph. Shaken, they rode on and came upon the estate, which turned out to be 112 acres, considerably larger than the stipulated forty.

After much thought and discussion, the purchase of the mansion and the property was concluded at the astounding sum of about $65,000. On February 11, 1926, the Sisters of Christian Charity acquired legal possession of the Cromwell property that would become the first motherhouse of the Sisters of Christian Charity of the North American Eastern Province."

—Sisters of Christian Charity

Charolais Farms, Cromwell Lane, Kerby Lane, and the Sisters of Christian Charity were one huge estate owned by Frederick Cromwell.

Cromwell's main estate house, known then as Ellis Court, is familiar to us today as the home of the Sisters of Christian Charity. According to John Turpin, co-author of *New Jersey Country Houses—The Somerset Hills*, the Cromwells were decedents of the English parliamentarian, Oliver Cromwell. He was treasurer and trustee of the Mutual Life Insurance Company for more than twenty years and served as the director of several railway transportation firms. He was known for his attention to landscaping and as a local philanthropist. In 1893 he funded a major expansion and renovation of St. Mark's Church, which included a new pipe organ.

We think a moment about how Mr. Cromwell would have reacted upon knowing that one of his trees made its way from the Sisters of Christian Charity to Rockefeller Center in 1995 and was lighted on national television.

As we stop to water our horses at the intersection of Bernardsville and Pleasant Valley Roads, we are but a short ride to many of the Gilded Age mansions that Mr. Turpin described in his books. If we could see up the hill and through the trees, we might see Mr. Cromwell leaving Ellis Court and traveling through a back path to visit his son, Seymore, who lives at what was the one hundred-acre Cromwell Cottage Estate. Seymore Cromwell's estate became known to many Mendhamites through the years as the Sandrellan Estate, even though the property changed hands many times.

Seymore Cromwell was given Cromwell Cottage by his father in 1914. Seymore was president of the New York Stock Exchange in 1921, one of the founders of the Better Business Bureau, and he was awarded the Legion of Honor by the French government for his work with French orphans. His wife, Agnes M. Whitney, was the first woman to serve on the New Jersey State Board of Education. After Frederick Cromwell's death in 1923, Seymore and his wife moved to Ellis Court and transferred title of Cromwell Cottage to Kate Harrison and John Hill Prentice. John Prentice's sister was married to E. H. Talmage. Today Prentice Lane borders the estate on the west side.

In 1945 Merrell Kerby Saunders purchased the one hundred-acre estate that was Cromwell cottage. He kept the land on which the original country manor was built and called it Sandrellan, Gaelic for "Saunders Land." The other portion of the land is today's Kerby Lane. Saunders was an air-conditioning magnate. With his own business he held large-scale contracts for the Pentagon, the United Nations, Rockefeller Center, and the World Trade Center. In the 1940s his firm worked with physicist J. Robert Oppenheimer on development of the first atomic bomb during the Manhattan Project.

Oh no, another cow! In *Gone with the Wind*, Aunt Pittypat could not imagine that they had "Yankees in Georgia." Could you imagine her reaction to French cows in Mendham? We had better return this one fast; it's a special breed. Just before the Nazi invasion of France, Saunders learned about a breed called Charolais—all-white cattle, they produce more beef than the North American Black Angus. After the war, Saunders brought Charolais cattle to the United States. At that time, each top-quality bull was worth about $100,000, and several roamed his Mendham property, now known as Charolais Farms.

Top: Cromwell Farms, with horses grazing, is believed to be the location of Charolais Farms, 1903. *Courtesy of Michael Smith*

Bottom: Cromwell Pond, located on the west side of Hilltop Road. Adjacent to the pond is the Thomas property, one of the largest remaining tracts in the borough, 1904. *Courtesy of Michael Smith*

Bliss Estate

Hold the horses steady now! Even with the advent of automobiles, we might have seen Mr. Bliss riding to the Bernardsville station in his horse-drawn carriage to catch the train to New York . . . . He drives the carriage at a fast pace and allows one of his drivers to return the team to his Bliss Road estate. Let's head up Bliss Road and imagine some more.

What we know today as Roxiticus Golf Club was once called Wendover, the estate of Walter Phelps Bliss. The original estate spanned six hundred acres in Mendham and Bernardsville, and the house was a thirty-nine-room mansion, one of the largest in the area. The Bliss home was completed in 1905. On the estate were formal gardens, a racetrack, a carriage house, brick horse stables, barns, greenhouses, tennis courts, and a gashouse. For many years, Bliss also had his own dairy herd. We also heard that Rudolf Valentino, motion picture idol of the 1920s, worked as a gardener on the Bliss estate when he first came to the United States from Italy. After playing a role as an extra in "Four Horsemen of the Apocalypse," he became a well known actor.

Good thing we are riding in carriages and on horseback. Look at that sign: "Absolutely no autos allowed." Bliss does not want this newfangled invention on his property, but we hear that is changing since our village doctor, Dr. De Groot, explained to him that automobiles were faster and more dependable if he had to reach a patient quickly.

Mr. Bliss died prematurely at the age of fifty-three in 1924 on a train headed to his New York office. Mrs. Bliss lived in the home until just before her death thirty years later.

Had we been on this hill in 1979, we would have witnessed history disintegrate in a tragic fire that destroyed the Roxiticus Golf Club clubhouse, the

Top left: The view across what was once Cromwell's duck pond.

Top right: A giant evergreen is cut and loaded on a flatbed at Mallinckrodt, Sisters of Christian Charity. Destination: New York City. *Sisters of Christian Charity*

Bottom left: Ellis Court from above. The home of Frederick Cromwell was converted for use by the Sisters of Christian Charity. *Sisters of Christian Charity*

Bottom right: A Mendham tree shines at New York's Rockefeller Center. *Sisters of Christian Charity*

Chapter Three: A Walk through Our Neighborhoods

old Bliss Mansion. Tragically, two people lost their lives when high winds rendered the fire out of control before the several responding fire departments arrived. Two hundred firefighters responded with twenty trucks. The hoses stretched for miles. One hundred thousand gallons of water from the swimming pool in the rear courtyard were used, to no avail, and rains from the previous day and night left the grounds too soggy for the heavy equipment to reach two large nearby ponds. Only the brick exterior and huge chimneys remained standing after the fire. The carriage house was undamaged.

Had we been on this hill in 1987, we would have seen a flight instructor and his student, who were practicing emergency maneuvers, safely crash-land a Cessna 152-II on the 18th fairway.

Balbrook Estate

Passing by Balbrook Road, we recall the land located between Pleasant Valley Road, Bliss Road, and Bernardsville Road as owned by Edward Balbrook Jr., who built an estate called Balbrook in 1891. The Balbrook family were industrialists who believed in education for skilled workers. They were financial supporters and contributors to an initiative that eventually became the New Jersey Institute of Technology.

Oakdine Estate

Quickly we approach Oakdine, also built during the 1890s, by Charles W. Ide, president of the New York Cotton Exchange. His wife, Fannie Ogden Ide, was an author of children's books under the pen name Ruth Ogden. The home was sold to the Pyle family, who operated a soap company that developed Pearline, once the most popular washing powder in the country (acquired by Procter & Gamble Company in 1914). They lived in the home for twenty-two years. Since then, the home has been used as a school for boys, a church, a children's summer camp, and a religious-counseling center. Today it is again a private residence. A fire in 1990 destroyed much of the original structure.

Top: The Balbrook Estate. *Courtesy of Don Preziosi*

Bottom: Today's mansions cover much of the old Cromwell Estate, as seen from the Sisters of Christian Charity property. *Photo by Michael Gaffney*

Woodmere Farms

It must have been quite a thrill to be invited to a party at Tollemache House, also known as White Pillars, the summer residence of Edward G. Talmage. He and his wife, Mary Prentice, hosted many social events at the home built in 1894, inviting people from Park Avenue to Tuxedo Park. The home even had an underground kitchen in which the coachmen and grooms could eat and rest.

Talmage worked for the Delaware, Lackawanna & Western Railroad and was a member of the New York Stock Exchange. He loved animals and established the first Bernardsville Horse Show in 1902. Talmage died at the age of fifty-five, but his widow stayed on at Woodmere Farms. In early 1926 she removed two wings from the house, leaving it with twelve rooms. The wings were used to build another house located on the estate.

The four hundred-acre estate on which it resided was called Woodmere Farms. It stretched all the way from Bernardsville Road to Talmage Road and yet again across that street. As we return to the twenty-first century, White Pillars no longer exists, but the memories do.

We have asked special permission of the Horseshoe Bend Road residents to use their private road and cross the Talmage Estate on the way back to town. As we turn, we nod a pleasant afternoon to our second mayor of Mendham Borough, Dean Sage, who purchased the land for his home from Talmage. Sage was not only a mayor, but a lawyer and philanthropist. He was also an amateur zoologist who led one of the first expeditions to China in search of the giant panda. He was named president of New York Presbyterian Hospital in 1922 and had the honor of announcing the plans to build Columbia–Presbyterian Medical Center.

Leisurely riding down the winding, tree-lined Cherry Lane, we can still see Three Fields, the home of Andrew Fletcher. The home, located on a fifty-acre parcel and originally part of the Talmage Estate, was built in 1929, purchased by Fletcher in 1949, and donated by him to the borough in 1965.

Even while serving as president and CEO of the St. Joseph Lead Corporation, Fletcher contributed to the civic and charitable well-being of the community. He served as councilman and mayor from 1957 to 1964. In addition to serving as a trustee and board president of the library, Fletcher left the library a grant to build and maintain a new wing that was later named in his honor. This grant continues to provide funding to the library. In addition to all their other considerations, the Fletchers gifted their home to the borough. The borough, retaining a life interest in the residence, sold the property after the couple's deaths and now retains the fund to be used for the good of the community.

Left: The Dean Sage Estate, once part of the Talmage Estate. *Mendham Borough archives*

Right: At the owner's direction, the Andrew Fletcher Estate was donated to the borough after his death. It was sold at auction, with the proceeds placed in a fund for the benefit of borough taxpayers. In addition, Fletcher endowed the borough library. *Mendham Borough archives*

Chapter Three: A Walk through Our Neighborhoods   75

Audley Farms

Riding up Prentice Lane, we are now at Talmage Road and can see Audley Manor. The estate of Edward Talmage's younger brother, John F. Talmage, was called Audley Farms. About 270 acres, it was located next to that of his brother and ran approximately from the south side of Cherry Lane, across Talmage Road until it reached the Franklin Murphy property. Audley Manor is located on a hill on the south side of Talmage Road with wonderful views of Hilltop Church and the north. A working farm, the estate had many outbuildings, such as an aviary, greenhouses, chicken and pheasant runs, and a cow barn.

The barn and other outbuildings, known as the "chicken coops," were converted to homes and featured in a 1920 book titled *Beautiful Homes of Morris County*. Along with the manor house, they are a reminder of the magnitude of the estate. A huge barn, once used as a horse riding stable, stood across the road from the manor house. When the property was sub-divided, the barn was removed to make way for the new homes. If you live on Coventry and Demarest Roads, you walk the fields that surrounded the old barn.

After the Talmages left the estate in 1937, the now-private residence was used as Miss Gill's School until 1940.

Top left: Outbuildings on the Talmage Estate were converted to homes—"the chicken coops." *Mendham Borough archives*

Top right: The Thomas Lowery farmhouse, located on Talmage Road, was rebuilt in its likeness after fire destroyed the original structure. *Mendham Borough archives*

Bottom: One of the borough's finest: The Blachley home, at the corner of Cherry and Talmage. *Courtesy of Michas Family*

Left: The Hilltop Church stables before they were destroyed by fire.

Right: Returning home up the hill and across the fields to Hilltop Church.
Mendham Borough archives

Lowery Farms

Look at that lovely Victorian farmhouse! It is the Queen Anne-style home of the Lowery family on "the Lowery Farm." It was originally built in 1892. Destroyed by fire in 1983, the home was reconstructed in its original design. The property of the Lowery Farm was subdivided, enabling the development on Lowery Lane and Colville Drive.

Back to 2006

Heading back up the hill, we pass the stables at Hilltop Church and move toward the center of town. As we once again enter the village center, we encounter a twenty-first-century traffic jam as children are being picked up at Hilltop School for the day. It provides us with a little time to reminisce and think about how education has been an integral part of borough culture since earliest times.

It's getting late now, so let's drop the horses and carriage off at Gunther's. If we hurry, we still have time stop for an ice cream soda at Robinson's. If we're not too tired, we might even catch a movie at the town hall. At least, we could have years ago —neither movies nor ice cream cones are available to us in "modern" Mendham.

North, South, East, or West, we have been able to see the diverse group of people that have come together in one way or another to share history and contribute in varying ways to Mendham, to helping each other, and to society. It is what has made Mendham . . . Our Home . . . the one thing that has not changed.

Chapter Three: A Walk through Our Neighborhoods

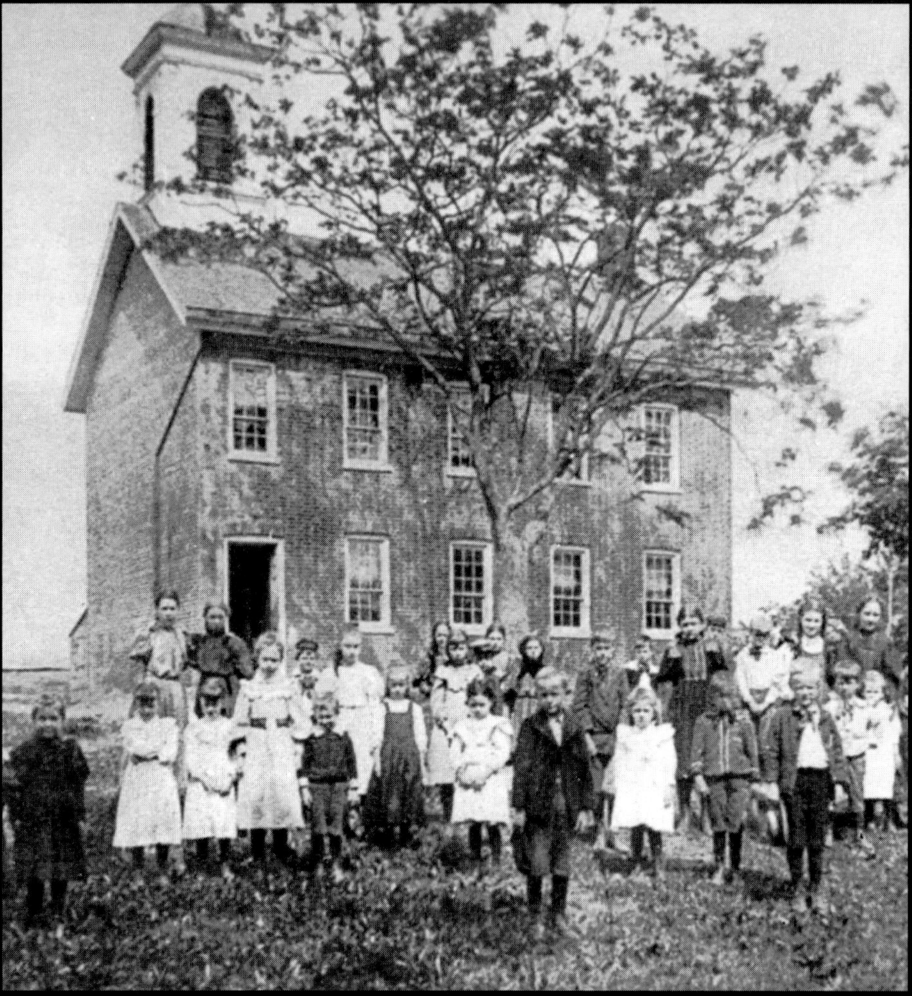

Chapter Four
Educating Our Children

*Education is when you read the fine print.
Experience is what you get if you don't.*

—Pete Seeger

The Early Schools

Waiting for the light at our crossroads during rush hour, one almost invariably notices any number of children coming to or from school. If you live close to the village center, you can walk to any number of nursery schools, move on to Hilltop School, graduate from Mountain View, and attend Mendham High School without the need for wheeled transport of any type. (Yes, we know that unwritten laws require everyone over the age of fourteen to drive or be driven to high school—regardless of the proximity of their home.) If you prefer a nonsecular school, feel free to take the thirty-second walk down West Main to St. Joseph's.

The borough remains properly proud of its educational system. From the earliest schools to the proliferation of pre-kindergarten schools through the building of West Morris Mendham High School, there has been a history of excellent educational options available to Mendham students. In the 1700s most of the "book learning" was offered in private homes either by parents or, for those who could afford it, by paid clergymen and tutors; but records show that as early as the 1790s, more formal schooling was offered.

Credit for establishing the first school generally goes to Dr. Henry Axtell, who opened his "Red

One of many area nursery schools, the Mendham Cooperative Nursery School celebrates its forty-third year during a Labor Day parade. *Courtesy of Carolyn Menagh*

Top left: Hilltop Class of 1950 (not in order): F. David Ayers, Bruce Dunham, Mildred Garabrant, Courtland Guerin III, Patricia Gunther, Joseph Havas, Carlton Hippchen, Jacob Lewis Jr., Peter Many, Richard Menagh, Kenneth Ort, Alice Parrillo, Joan Parrillo, Theresa Parrillo, Spencer Potter. *Mendham Borough Library archives*

Top right: Borough school staff, 1947: back row (l-r) Mrs. Stoll, Mrs. Watkins, Mrs. Garabrant, Mrs. Farley, Mrs. Hopper, Miss Treible, Mr. Vold. Front row (l-r) Mrs. Rooney, Mrs. Belton, Mr. Weinhold (principal), Miss Ferguson, Miss Lowery. *Mendham Borough Library archives*

Bottom: Students in front of Hilltop School, 1800s. *Mendham Borough Library archives*

Brick Academy" in a home built in 1795 and located at 17 Hilltop Road—part of a tract of land on which Hilltop Elementary School currently sits. Kate Emmons' research attributes the original "Hilltop School" as having been located first at the Phoenix House as early as 1824 and directed by Ezra Fairchild. Hilltop relocated in the late 1800s to the "Axtell" school at the present location.

At any time during the 1800s, there were as many as six private schools located in the village. One, the Rankin School, charged $75 tuition and board for a thirteen-week session. The quality education is reflected by the fact that Dr. Rankin is credited for preparing 76 students for college, 150 for teaching, 50 for the clergy, 30 as lawyers, and an additional 12 who became medical doctors.

Other schools operating locally in the 1800s included the Mendham Female Seminary administered by M. M. Liddell (1876), Leila and Mary Babbitt's School, located first at 5 Prospect Street and later at 18 West Main Street (1881–1901), and the Dodd's School, situated at the site of the St. Mark's parish house (1860s).

Hilltop around 1950. *Courtesy of Marie Griffin*

Remembering Hilltop before renovations: mural adorned the hallway. *Courtesy of Marie Griffin*

Morristown Class of 1909 on their Washington trip. About a dozen are Mendham students who attended. *Courtesy of Mrs. De Vore*

Schoolboy Pranks

Walking through the graveyard at the First Presbyterian Hilltop Church, one might notice the record of a feat of longevity not often matched. The headstone for William Beers, who died in 1790, reads "Aged 237 Years and 3 Months and 24 Days." He died at age twenty-three, but according to reports, the addition of the "7" is a result of a talented student chiseler. The miscreant appears to have been a student of Dr. William Rankin, but despite the great hullabaloo in the village when the prank was discovered, no names were named. The act likely occurred between 1850 and 1875 and when discovered, the tombstone was cast aside. When the cemetery was improved in 1921, the stone was resurrected and replaced in the cemetery but most likely not on the spot where Beers is actually buried.

Daniel Beers' gravestone at Hilltop Cemetery shows he died at age 237 years—a schoolboy prank. *Mendham Borough Library archives*

After the Common School Act of 1829 established the means for a public school system, public education became more prevalent. William Rankin became superintendent of the Mendham Township Schools in 1847, and by 1883 the munificent sum of $589.75 in tax dollars was appropriated to the Mendham School system.

In the general area of the Hilltop School, continued expansion took place until the present Hilltop School was built in 1928–29. By 1929 the budget rose to $24,525 for the year, and given the outstanding results on state examinations, the cost was deemed to be a worthwhile investment.

Of course, the quality of the teachers has a major effect on the caliber of education, and perhaps no teacher was remembered more fondly than Miss Elizabeth Oliver.

The Borough Schools

At the Hilltop School in 1934, there were some 213 students in grades one through the third year of high school. For their senior year, students attended Morristown High, transported daily on James Menagh's bus. By 1940, Hilltop became entirely a grade school, and everyone spent four years at Morristown High.

Hilltop was expanded in 1957 (and again just recently), but by 1966 more space was required, and Mountain View Middle School was opened. Finally, in 1970 West Morris Mendham High School opened.

Moving from Hilltop to Mountain View, a short walk but always perceived as a traumatic experience, forced one from the warm, fuzzy protection of lower-school teachers to face a new environment (and the "big kids") under the guidance of a new set of teachers and counselors.

From 1960 to 2005 part of the new guidance responsibilities fell to Doris Mills. Few, if any, educators can speak to our school system as can Mills:

"High standards, excellence, tradition seems to be the keywords when one considers the Mendham Borough Schools. A small school district where everyone knows everyone by name, where teachers are more than caring, where parents are more

The Oliver Sisters

On February 9, 1956, the Pastime Club hosted a surprise eighty-third birthday party for Miss Mary Elizabeth Oliver. Despite inclement weather, some three hundred people celebrated the occasion by attending the "This is Your Life" show at the Hilltop School. Miss Oliver taught in the Mendham school system for more than thirty-six years. She lived with her sister, Eva, a nurse, and both ladies were described as being loved and respected by the community. They were unselfish volunteers for the Methodist Church, Campfire Girls, and Boy Scouts.

---

than involved, where community support is constant, the Mendham Borough Schools are recognized as outstanding and special. Many alumni leave to pursue their educations and careers, but return to raise their families in the community and the school system.

"Mickey Fagan and Marie Pennimpede, who have lived in the Borough all their lives, shared with me recollections of the early days of the Borough School. The original building was built about 1930, and perhaps twenty years later, two wings were added, which included a home economics room, a wood shop, and a library, as well as a number of classrooms. Lunches of sandwiches, soup, and dessert were prepared by the home economic classes and sold to students for 15 cents. Eventually, Mrs. Watkins became the cafeteria manager and cook until Marie Pennimpede replaced her. In home economic classes, the girls made their graduation dresses and one year made a complete layette for a needy family. Mr. A. Seeley Hutchinson was a beloved principal who was shared with the Township and who walked from one school to the other on a regular basis.

There was no foreign language taught in the early days; music, art, and physical education courses were taught by classroom teachers.

"When I arrived in Mendham in 1960, there was one K-8 school. Principal Bill Satterlee had just left, and Joe Tiscornia took over the helm. Teachers in 1960 included Loretta Rooney, Frances Garabrant, Katherine Farley, Dick Johnston, Dick Joubert, Mimi Woodruff, Pat Taylor, Frank Marrapodi, Jack Van Deursen, Joe Kienzle, and Allan Johnson, who arrived with me that year—all of whom remained in the Borough Schools until their retirements. Mrs. Rooney and Mrs. Garabrant retired in the early '60s, having taught together at the second grade level for many years. They are honored by the Mendham Borough Education Association Garabrant-Rooney Scholarship. It is awarded

The Oliver Sisters: Mary Elizabeth (left) and Eva. *Mendham Borough Library archives*

Doris Mills, social studies teacher 1960–1987, guidance counselor 1985–2005. *Courtesy of Doris Mills*

to a graduating senior from the West Morris Regional High School student who plans a career in education.

"This was the beginning of one of the traditions. Funds for the Garabrant-Rooney Scholarship were raised through a basketball game, at first played by male faculty members against the boys' varsity team. The whole staff was involved, serving refreshments and selling raffle tickets. As time went on, the men got older and the boys did not; the game then became a homecoming pitting high school freshmen against the boys' varsity team. The Garabrant-Rooney Scholarship game has morphed into the annual Blue and Gold game including both boys' and girls' teams; money is still raised for the scholarship awarded annually to a Mendham High School senior.

"Another tradition that began in the '60s was the Eighth Grade Fair, created to support an existing tradition—the Washington trip. Two students, Lynn Bruen and Brenda Beavers, contacted me during the summer with the idea of having an Eighth Grade Fair; they had thought their idea through and had a plan: bake sale, white elephants, homemade games. The first fair netted about $800, and I am sure many treasures found in the drawers and closets of Mendham were sold for a nickel or a dime. The fair continues as an important community event held the first Saturday in October and has become a very exciting and sophisticated day for which parents spend months planning. Thousands are raised each year.

"The Washington trip, another important tradition in Mendham Borough, had been a highlight of the eighth or ninth grade year for as long as anyone can remember. At our senior citizens' luncheon each May, often occurring the Monday after we returned from the trip, our seniors who grew up in the community fondly recall their trip, which were suspended only during the World War II years. While the school still housed ninth-graders, it was they who went to Washington. In 1960 and for many years previously, the trip was a two-day trip; parents drove their youngsters to Princeton Junction, usually in March, sometimes in wintry weather, where they boarded a train for the nation's capital. The trip quickly became a three-day trip, traveling by bus; there are many sites and more being added each year. The present trip includes breakfast with our Congressman, a theater experience, often a wreath-laying ceremony in Arlington National Cemetery, and a full itinerary. It is still a highlight of our students' eighth grade year as well as of their total experience in our schools. In the '30s, our students wore dresses, hats, gloves, and jackets and ties; as of 2005, our students wear dresses/skirts, jackets/ties. Other schools have asked, "How do you do it?" and we have replied, "Our parents support us." I recall a parent writing me a note thanking me for continuing the dress code (this might have been in the '70s), saying, 'I never thought I'd see my son in a jacket and tie, but as long as his friends were doing it, he was into it. He walked proudly on the bus to Washington, D.C.'

"There were many memorable moments from the Washington Trips. While attending a performance of 'Anna Christie' at the Washington National Theater, the players on the stage suddenly stepped out of character and turned to look up at a box as President and Mrs. Carter arrived to enjoy the performance. The entire

Top: Teacher Marie Griffin leads the traditional Halloween Parade, 1981.

Bottom: Now retired, Dave Garrison lends his expertise to a Mountain View soccer team. He was a physical education teacher and soccer, basketball, and baseball coach as well as town recreation director, and decades of young men grew up with and benefited from his coaching.

assemblage stood and broke out in sustained and enthusiastic applause. Our students were thrilled beyond description. On another occasion, we caught a glimpse of Queen Elizabeth II on her visit to Washington. We went on our trip within days of the Martin Luther King assassination and were chilled to witness National Guardsmen protecting all of our national shrines with bayonets and rifles. And then there was the time when one of our students dutifully hung her garment bag on a hook in a Hyatt hotel room as we were preparing to leave the hotel on our final day when suddenly cascades of water overflowed the room; she had hung her bag on a newly installed sprinkler system. To this day, the Hyatt has a notice warning guests not to hang anything on the hook. The hotel has continued to welcome us back for many years since and graciously noted that the incident was a good test of the new sprinkling system!

"Can anyone forget 'Bye, Bye, Birdie'? We always had a wonderful music program—bands, strings, choruses, delightful concerts. When music teacher Nancy Holland arrived in the '70s and saw our talented student body, she became a Mickey Rooney: 'Let's put on a show!' The whole staff rallied. We spent hours on tryouts and discussions about casting and brought Broadway to Mendham. Students, grades 4–8 discovered talents they did not know they had and went on to successful careers in opera and show business. There have been many shows since that involved staff members who are eager to give our students opportunities for their futures. At the time, there is a show every other year starring seventh and eighth graders both on the stage and behind the scenes and a talent show every other year.

Top left: Mendham Borough School, entire 1907 enrollment. *Courtesy of Mendham Fire Department*

Top right: The Hilltop Auditorium, 1980. Public reaction against the eventual renovations included objections to losing both the old auditorium with its wooden chairs and the sledding hill behind the school. *Courtesy of Marie Griffin*

Bottom: Hilltop School property when there were two schools. The building on the left was the former Bogart Chapel purchased by the new school district in 1914. *Courtesy of Kate Emmons,* Through the Years in Mendham Borough

Miss Mills mentions the flooding of the Hyatt hotel on the Mountain View eighth grade trip. Who hung her garment bag on the sprinkler system "hook," and what is she doing now?

Answer: Star Moran—she teaches elementary school.

Chapter Four: Educating Our Children 85

Left: Advertising the eighth grade fair. A Fundraiser for the Washington, D.C., trip.

Right: The 1941 Outhouse Caper. As told by Johnny Enright, Tom Emmons, Johnny Grassi, and an unidentified group of other schoolboys moved Jim Farrell's outhouse from his property on East Main Street to the center of town. This was the second attempt—on the first try, it was occupied by its owner. Drawing by B. Haslam. *Courtesy of John Enright*

"Over the years, eighth grade career expositions and sixth grade science fairs have given our students opportunities to explore their interests and demonstrate their learning. The three-day environmental education trip for sixth graders has given them lessons not only in the environment but also in sharing, trusting, and getting along. At Hilltop, the annual Halloween parade brings delight to the parents and the community.

"Traditions are important but the nuts and bolts of a school system are in the curriculum and the day-to-day delivery of the curriculum . . . . The path is established at Hilltop and carried through at Mountain View—small classes, individual attention, teams of teachers working together. Meeting the needs of learning-disabled students as well as academically talented students has also drawn recognition and appreciation to our schools. When others did not, we had foreign languages— first French, then French and Spanish, now Spanish only. When others did not, we had home economics and wood shop. A step into the Mountain View gym shows the visitor the many championship banners won by boys' and girls' teams at the county level. Aside from the strong physical education program and athletic prowess, the foyer of the Mountain View is full of trophies won by students in Mind Bowl, Brain Bowl, forensics, spelling and geography bees, and other activities for the gifted and talented . . . . Former students reading this may recall with pride our winning the national championship in Newscope, a weekly current events challenge. Opportunities in art and exhibits in many art media in both schools show how much students' talents are discovered and developed.

"Over the years there have been administrators with long tenures who had a positive influence on the tone and character of our schools. In addition to Mr. Hutchinson and Mr. Satterlee, Dr. Leo Poulos served from 1970 to 1985. Edith Von der Heiden was principal of Hilltop School and continued to serve as principal of the Regional Day School when the Borough oversaw its operation. Bob Marold was principal of Mountain View for eighteen years and is now principal of Hilltop School. Many administrators have come and gone, but these provided a steady hand, consistency, and stability for many years.

"'Something for every student' has been our unspoken goal: providing enough and varied activities so that each student can find a niche—or many niches—where

Left: The front of West Morris Mendham High School showing the Julius Wargacky Memorial Garden in the foreground. The well-respected teacher and administrator passed away prematurely not long after being named principal.

he or she can find outlets for those talents and ambitions buried deep within him or her. Meeting the individual needs of our students in the academics through varying activities and materials has been essential to their successes. When our students move on to high school, we and their parents look upon them with pride, knowing that they have the skills to succeed, not only in the classroom but on the stage, the courts, the fields, the meeting rooms. Our alumni do return to raise their children in the community and school system. We should be proud—and we are!"

Doris Mills retired in 2005 after serving the borough schools and leading its students for forty-five years; a social studies teacher from 1960–87, she served as a guidance counselor from 1985 to 2005.

West Morris Mendham High School

Home to about twelve hundred students, West Morris Mendham High School has achieved all expectations and continues to flourish.

Since the 1800s, the land upon which the high school stands, a highly cherished spot, has had only a few owners. Its first major proprietor, Jerome Stout, a general farmer, owned the land from 1840 to 1875. As one of the wealthiest men in town, Stout was able to fully preserve the land up to the Presbyterian Church, Hilltop Elementary School, and New Street. To many, he was known as one of the most influential men in the area.

Above left: Texas may have its Friday night lights, but Mendham has Friday night hoops and a championship tradition.

Above right: Molly Creamer going to the hoop. After Mountain View School, Molly played on the Mendham High Team that went 32–0 in 1998, winning the New Jersey State Tournament of Champions. In college she showed she really had game by becoming the leading scorer (female or male) in Bucknell and Patriot League history. A Division I All-American, she has played professionally in Israel and France. *Courtesy of Chris Creamer*

Chapter Four: Educating Our Children **87**

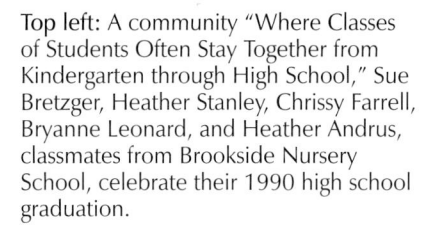

Top left: A community "Where Classes of Students Often Stay Together from Kindergarten through High School," Sue Bretzger, Heather Stanley, Chrissy Farrell, Bryanne Leonard, and Heather Andrus, classmates from Brookside Nursery School, celebrate their 1990 high school graduation.

Top right: Teacher Henry Bullock. *Courtesy of Sharon Hakakian*

Bottom left: *Teacher Barbara Nutt. Courtesy of Sharon Hakakian*

Bottom right: For the past quarter-century, Mendham High basketball coaches have put together a record rarely equaled. In twenty-six years through the 2005 season, boys coach Jim Baglin (r) has 537 wins and 147 losses. In twenty-five years, now retired protégé and girls coach Fred Corona was 503–159. *Courtesy of Fred Corona*

Ten years after Stout left the land, Edward Elliott moved in and stayed until 1924. In 1906, when the borough incorporated, Elliott became the first mayor of the borough. Widely known as the "big kahuna," Elliott owned one hundred acres of land and three sawmills and was the richest and most politically connected individual in Mendham Borough. In 1924 the property's third major owner, the Cullen family, developed one of the most prosperous dairy farms in the area.

Later, Lawrence Lawry and his brother-in-law, Mr. Rowbottom, bought the land and divided it. In 1948 Harold Traudt and the Rowe family became the last official major proprietors before the land was needed to build the high school. The remaining eight acres is now owned by Peter Rowe and his brother.

In recent years, West Morris Mendham was ranked fourth in the state in *New Jersey Monthly* magazine and was later recognized as one of the top one thousand high schools (140th) across the nation by *Newsweek*. Students at Mendham have maintained high expectations as they consistently receive such awards as the National Merit Scholarship and the Edward J. Bloustein Distinguished Scholar award. They continue to excel in a variety of areas, including more than seventeen subjects for which advanced placement classes are offered. Mendham is one of only a few high schools in New Jersey to offer the International Baccalaureate Program, and the list of college acceptances reflects the quality of education.

Mendham's academic programs are matched by the athletic teams, as evidenced by the fact that there appears to be little remaining space left in the gymnasium to hang additional banners reflecting championships on the league, county, and state levels. Friday night hoops have become a Mendham tradition, and virtually all athletic programs have had outstanding successes.

The school district's Long Range Plan is to provide "an intellectually challenging experience that promotes a passion for learning, academic excellence, involved citizenship, and personal responsibility."

St. Joseph's School

The idea for a parish center and school for St. Joseph's parishioners is credited to Father Hewetson, who initiated the planning in 1954. The men of the parish's Holy Name Society embraced the need to build a parish center for religious instruction, and they volunteered not only to raise the funds, but to assist in the center's construction.

Over a three-year period, some $56,000 was raised to purchase building materials. With a strong hands-on approach, the center was dedicated on June 7, 1957. The bishop of Paterson, the Most Reverend James A. McNulty, administered the blessing and dedication of what would become the original St. Joseph's School. In the cornerstone, there is a copper box that contains the names of the men and women who eventually donated a total of $200,000 for the original construction.

During the sixties and seventies, the Mendhams experienced a surge in the construction of new homes, and St. Joseph's joined the ranks of local citizens in meeting the educational needs of the young with the construction of an elementary school. Groundbreaking for the two-story, eight-classroom building took place in 1962 and was dedicated in June 1963. The school opened with the Missionary Sisters of the Immaculate Conception of the Mother of God administering and teaching. The first eighth grade class graduated in 1968. Around 1970 a crisis arose when the sisters no longer had sufficient numbers to staff the school, but the Sisters of Christian Charity at Mallinckrodt stepped in.

St. Joseph's School children collect clothing for 9/11 victims. *Courtesy of Barbara Nelson*

Although the parish school met the educational needs of its students for forty years, advances in technology, combined with more sophisticated educational techniques, made it clear in 2000 that in order to remain competitive, expansion of the school facility was no longer a luxury but a necessity. Plans were explored and approved for a new state-of-the-art addition designed by Gianforcaro Architects and Engineers, parishioners of St. Joseph, to expand existing services for both the school population as well as the catechetical needs of parishioner students attending other area schools. Groundbreaking for the addition took place in January 2003, and the project was completed in record time by the fall of the same year, making St. Joseph a "full-serve" Catholic parish.

Historically, all the school systems have shared facilities, both outdoor and in, within the school systems and with the borough. This spirit of cooperation has allowed for the development of social, recreational, and athletic programs that would not otherwise be available to portions of the student population.

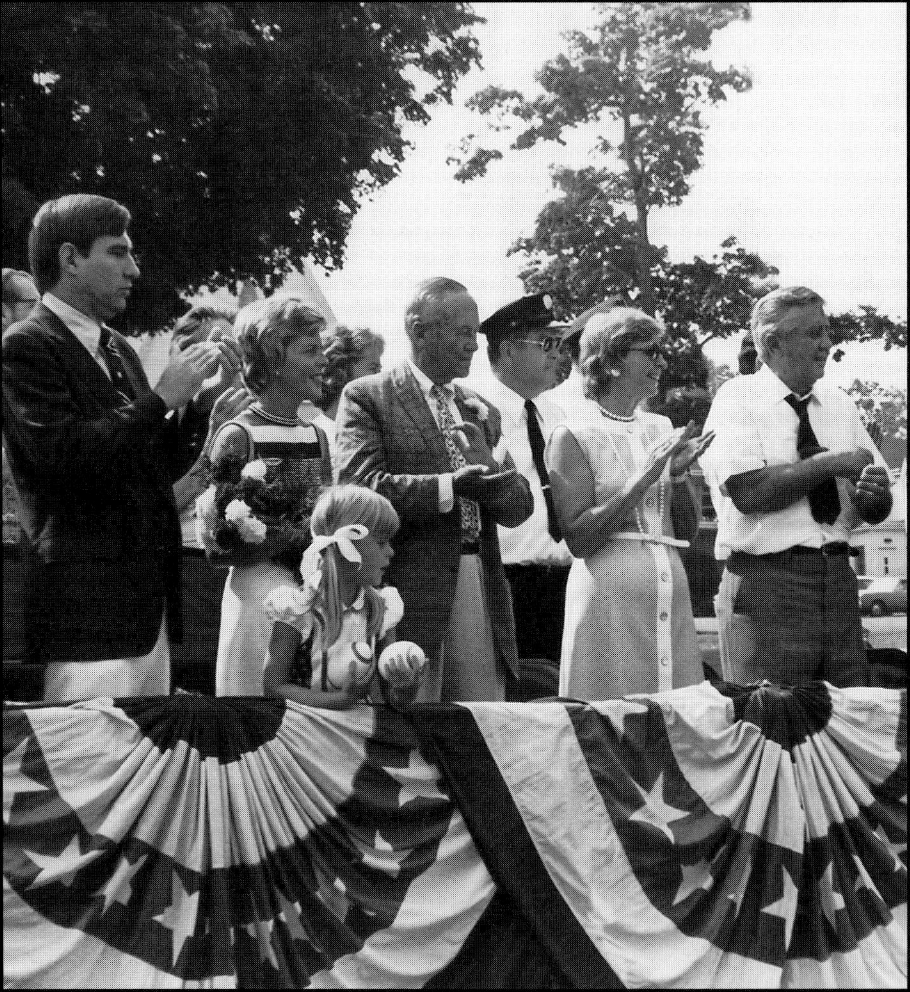

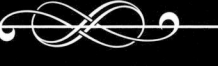

Chapter Five
Labor Day

Most importantly, the Pastime Club still runs the refreshment stand, profits are fed to the many sports organizations in town, and after a long summer, residents have an opportunity to reconnect with friends and neighbors.

The inaugural Labor Day celebration, now a borough tradition, took place in 1951. In conjunction with the borough's Recreation Committee, the Pastime Club sponsored races and games for all ages at the Mountain Valley Pool and the Borough Field. After prizes were awarded, there was a fireworks display, and during the day the Pastime Club operated a refreshment stand to raise funds. The first year was a notable success, and the tradition continued.

The parade was added, and the event eventually expanded to a full weekend extravaganza. As times have changed, children no longer grope with their feet for coin-loaded potatoes at the bottom of the pond, and there is no longer square dancing in the park, but games, rides, the fire department keg competition, concerts, and fireworks remain.

Most importantly, the Pastime Club still runs the refreshment stand, profits are fed to the many sports organizations in town, and after a long summer, residents have an opportunity to reconnect with friends and neighbors.

Residents celebrating Mendham Borough's one hundredth Anniversary

Most have forgotten that at one time the parade went from west to east on Main Street and was held on July Fourth. *Courtesy of Pat Serrano*

Antique cars have long been a part of the parade. Here they are displayed in front of the firehouse, 1980. *Courtesy of Mike Ackerman*

Junior Women's Club-sponsored races, 1981.

Sometimes riding, sometimes walking, the seniors have always been active participants.

Labor Day 2005—the fire department celebrates its one hundredth anniversary.

St. Joseph's School float, 2005.

93

The July 4, 1973, reviewing stand: (l-r) Mayor Bob Mulcahy, Terry Mulcahy, Muffin Mulcahy, Andrew Fletcher, Councilwoman Carol Gufstason. Councilman Jack Dormer, Fire Chief Jacob Lewis, Chief C. Everett Nelson, Department Chief Bob Quinlisk.
Courtesy of Terry Mulcahy

On parade day, Main Street is the place to be for brunch and parade watching.

Tennis tournament participants, 1999. Front: Russell Weinstein and Peter Janus. Back row: L. Matt Phillips, Jared Reback, Kevin Giblin, Manny Roderio, Chris Bailey, Todd Janus.

Three-on-three basketball competition; Matt "Chili" Soricelli drives to the hoop.

The Mendham Mops, early 1980s.

Postparade barrel competition— a fan favorite, 1975.

95

The Berenbaks enjoy a moment before parade kickoff. *Photo by Diana Callahan*

Retired Councilman Jerry Dolan enjoys the day as grand marshal of the 2005 parade. *Photo by John Andrus*

Steve Swiencki serves up a batch of fries for not the first time. *Courtesy of Bob Cleary*

A rare scene in the borough: a smiling Dave Crotsley and a content Tom Porter during the 2005 parade. *Photo by John Andrus*

Mayor Ackerman and wife, Peggy. Mike afforded Peggy many opportunities to pick up an annual bouquet. *Courtesy of Mike Ackerman*

The borough honors Frank Skidmore, who perished in the World Trade Center on 9/11/01. An active member at St. Joseph's Church, among many other volunteer efforts, Frank spent years marshaling the parade with the Knights of Columbus. Fr. Mike Drury drives as police officers Brian McNichol and Rich Morales form part of the honor guard.

Recreation Committee member Bob Sundt works to get the parade started on time. *Photo by Diana Callahan*

Two of Mendham's esteemed historians await the marchers at the corner of East Main and Hillcrest—Kate Emmons, whose book provided much of the historical information for this book, and Don Preziosi, who kindly offered his extensive postcard collection depicting many early Mendham scenes. *Photo by John Andrus*

Pastime Club members work the games. The Pastime share of the proceeds goes back into the community as funds to support various sports programs. *Courtesy of Bob Cleary*

Success is when you go home with the giant teddy. *Courtesy of Bob Cleary*

Sack races, 1987.

Wheelbarrow races. *Courtesy of Bob Cleary*

Lawnmower brigade precision drill team, 1982 parade.

A major fundraiser, the 50-50 pushes the $40,000 mark. *Courtesy of Bob Cleary*

Egg toss. *Courtesy of Bob Cleary*

Cover of Pastime Club program, 1983. *Courtesy of Bob Cleary*

Debbie Riescher and Lou Garubo work on a few steps during the fair. Early fairs had bands and a dance floor. Funds were raised at 25 cents per dance.

The First Aid Squad on call during the fireworks. *Courtesy of Bob Cleary*

101

Fr. Mike Drury's police clown-a-rounds. *Courtesy of Mendham Borough Police Department*

Mayor Kraft (rear) reviews his favorite band. The Funny Factory is a Labor Day favorite. *Courtesy of Ginnie Beutnagel*

The 2005 Labor Day parade recognizes the one hundredth anniversary of the borough fire department, as well as the first aid squad and police department. From left, Police Chaplain Fr. Mike Drury, Police Chief John Taylor, fire and first aid members Bob Raymond and Earl Barnes. Earl, a member of both departments for years, served as fire chief in 1974–75. The extended Barnes family, a mainstay of the borough, has provided the community with some of its finest volunteers, teachers, and athletes. Bob Raymond, also a longtime member of both squads, served as fire chief in 1996–97. In addition to fire call-outs, Bob responded to 299 first aid calls in 2004 and 298 first aid calls in 2005. No one could ask for a better neighbor. *Photo by Diana Callahan*

Labor Day weekend is often a time for old friends to reunite. For years softball standout Barry Abell dreamed about playing one last hardball game. It took place in 2000 when the old Jaycees took on the Little League Coaches. The agreed-upon "lob" pitching lasted about half an inning as the teams battled to a nine-inning 2-2 tie. Kneeling: Joe Miele, unknown, Paul Kelly, Mike Gaffney, Wayne LeBlond, Mark Bennett. Back and third row: Eric Keber, Chris Creamer, Rob Trout, Joe Arwady, Lou Allain, Fred Nicol, John Andrus, George Travis, Ron Riescher, Barry Abell, Jerry Jones, Lou Garubo, John Wilson.

Mainstays...

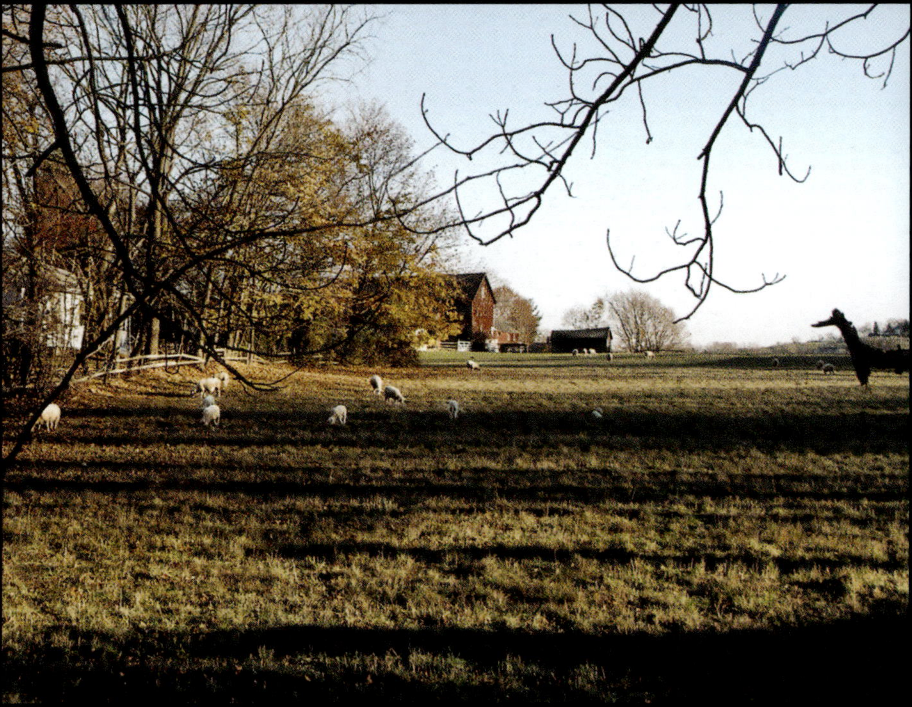

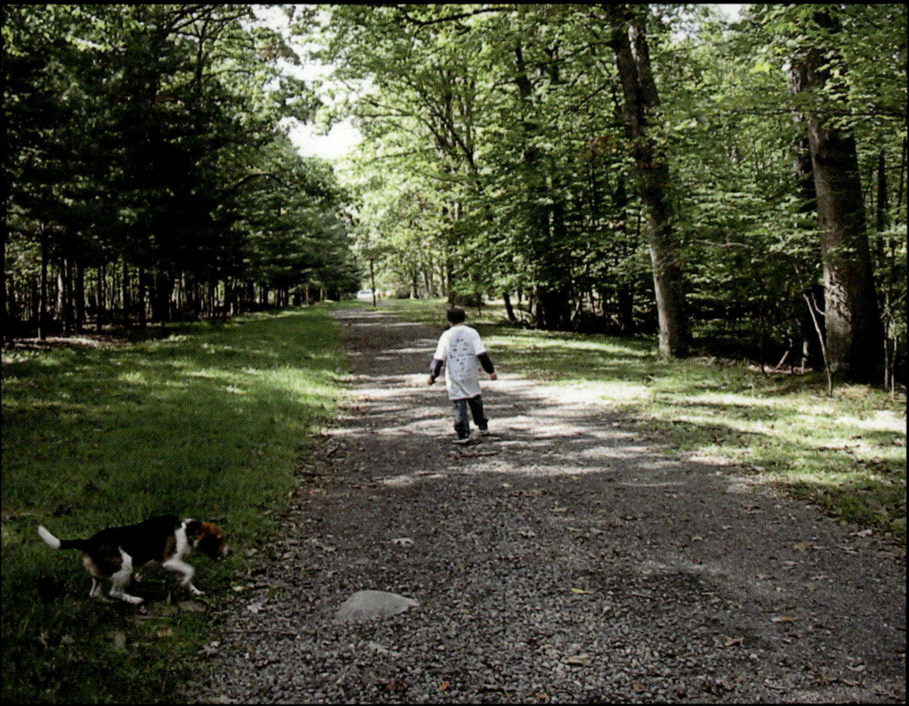

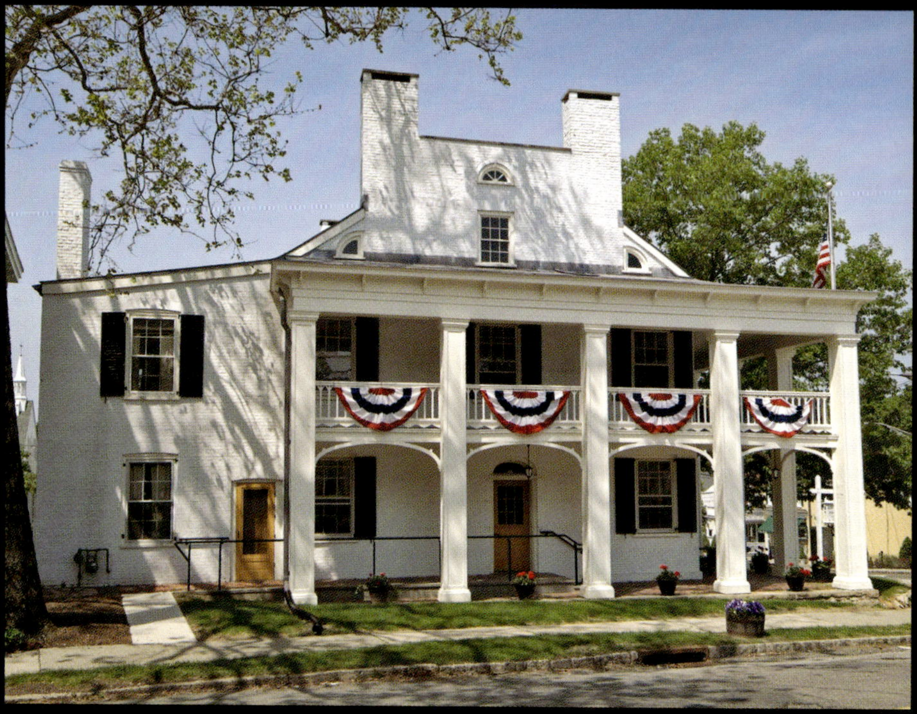

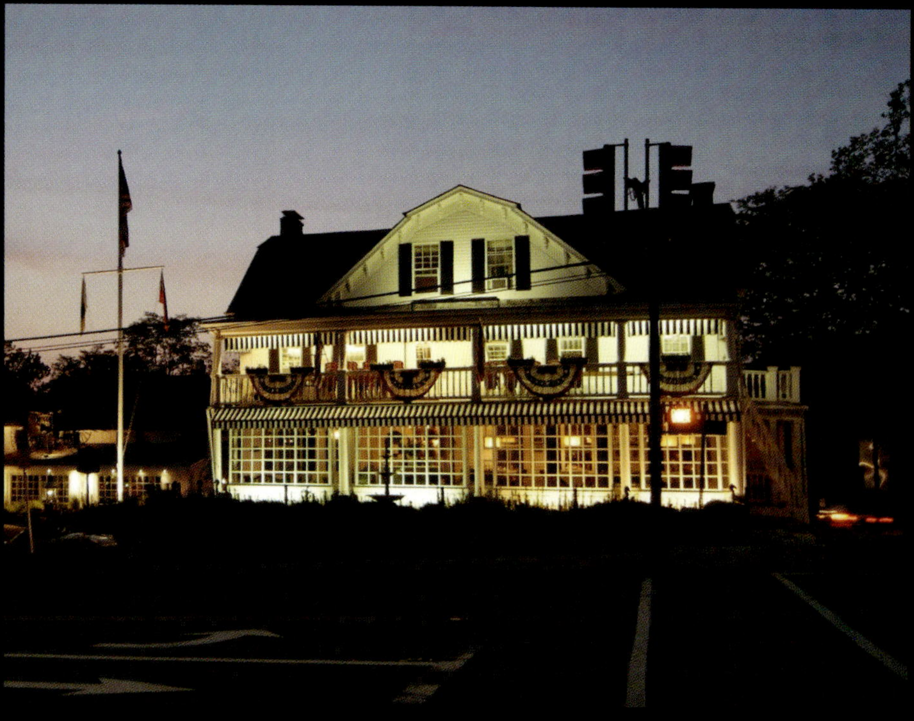

...of Mendham

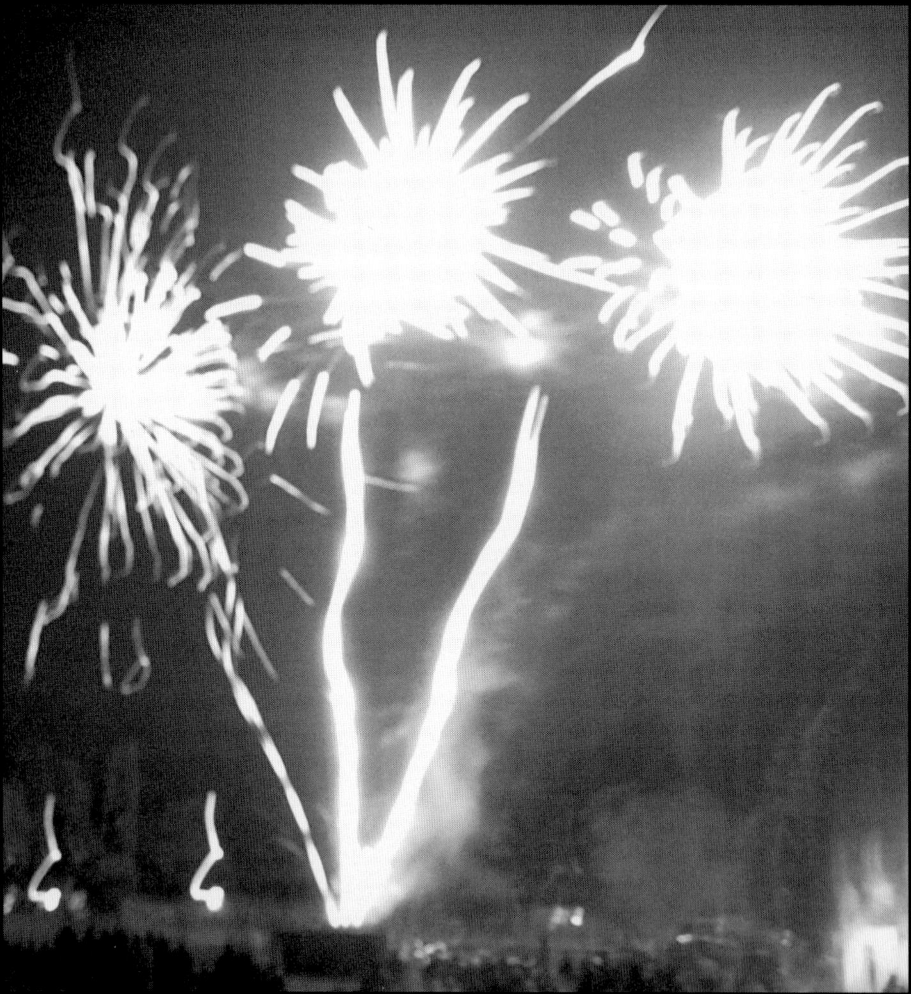

Chapter Six
The Centennial Celebration

The day began with a fishing derby at the stocked Mendham Valley Pool and ended with a fireworks display at the Borough Park.

On May 15, 2006, the Borough of Mendham officially celebrated its one hundredth anniversary with Mayor Richard Kraft presiding over a borough council meeting at the Phoenix House. After the mayor read proclamations commemorating the event, the meeting ended, and the overflow audience adjourned to a tented reception in the adjacent parking lot.

A time capsule buried twenty five years ago was unearthed from under the Phoenix House porch and opened. Among the contents were a copy of Bill Michas' calendar of sketches of Mendham scenes, poems written by borough students, various newspapers, and the like. Historian Kate Emmons attended, and her volume on the history of Mendham was displayed.

The reception preceded Saturday's old-fashioned Mendham Day. In an effort to honor the borough citizens, the council and recreation committee organized a full day's agenda. The day began with a fishing derby at the stocked Mendham Valley Pool and ended with a fireworks display at the Borough Park. In between were bike races up Mountain Avenue, a home run derby, tug-o'-wars, face painting, a pie-eating contest, hay rides, antique car show, and

Joe Ollerenshan and Gert Cronin dressed up for the antique car show.
Photo by Diana Callahan

109

Above: Centennial commemorative postcard designed by Don Preziosi and presented by the Mendham Borough Historical Society. *Courtesy of Don Preziosi*

Right: Mayor and Mrs. Kraft, Ruth Smith, Jim Bradley, and Barbara Nelson take a break. *Photo by Diana Callahan*

races and games. To keep the internal fires fueled, the Pastime Club manned the tent as the borough provided free burgers, dogs, soda, and ice cream. Long lines of consumers downed in one afternoon more than the Pastime Club serves during the four-day Labor Day weekend—obviously, the price was right.

Dinner included chicken, ribs, and shrimp, and the beer tent became popular as dusk settled. Friends could eat and drink all day while enjoying the music from no less than four bands, and most individuals sported badges displaying the year they moved to the borough. Nearly everyone left with the hope that the event could become an annual celebration.

Ally Marino takes second place in the pie-eating contest. *Photo by Bob Marino*

Above: Ice cream was free, and some was actually eaten. Cameron Boyle enjoys a treat.

Right: Anthony Orgera looking for ?

111

Micaela Fagan, one of the girls' winners in the Fishing Derby, concentrates as her father, Mike, observes.

Bike racers pedal up Mountain Avenue.

The first run for the tractor-pulled hay rides.

Historian Charles Topping gleefully anticipates getting his hands on the material from the time capsule for preservation in the Mendham Borough Library Archives. *Photo by John Andrus*

Kate Emmons, the borough's longest-living resident and historian, displays her history of the borough. *Photo by John Andrus*

The beer tent gained popularity as the evening progressed. The Otter Creek was the first to go.

113

Above: Bob Collins Jr. and Sr. enjoy the centennial. Both father and son have been active contributors to the borough. *Photo by John Andrus*

Left: Art Gillen hands out badges that residents wore with the date they moved to town.

Councilman Dave Murphy, Chief J. T. Taylor, Councilwoman Barbara Stanton, Councilman Neil Henry, and retired councilman John Andrus. *Photo by Diana Callahan*

Craig Bellamy, Ed Tencza, Mike Orgera, and Karen Bellamy Orgera enjoy some refreshments. *Photo by Diana Callahan*

Above: Two Daves—Murphy and Sharkey—enjoy (at least) two dogs.

Right: Residents and their children flocked to the Mountain Valley Pool for the Fishing Derby. The heavily stocked pond kept everyone in the tournament.

Mike Stewart, Cortez Ritchie, Pat Maynard, Mike Ackerman, Peter Kenny, Ruth Smith, and Barry Starke load the time capsule in 1976 prior to its burial under the Phoenix House porch. *Courtesy of Mike Ackerman*

On May 15, 2006, Mayor Kraft opens the capsule as Neil Henry looks on.

Wayne LeBlond, foreground, joins in perusing the contents of the time capsule.

Fireworks ended the evening.

Above: The dunking tank drew long lines.

Left: The pie-eating contest was so popular, it was difficult to get close enough to see. *Courtesy of Bob Marino*

117

Free hamburgers, hot dogs, soda, and ice cream drew long lines but very patient diners. The Pastime Club served, and in just a few hours, it surpassed the food consumption for all of Labor Day weekend.

The tug-o'-wars were popular events.

Rich Smith helps out at a table of longtime Mendham residents.

Centennial celebration schedule of events.

The Junior Women's Club sold personalized flags to raise funds and celebrate the centennial. The flags flew on Main Street, Mountain Avenue, and Hilltop Road. *Courtesy of Mike Gaffney*

Congressional Record

PROCEEDINGS AND DEBATES OF THE 109th CONGRESS, FIRST SESSION

House of Representatives

Vol. 152   WASHINGTON, Tuesday, May 2, 2006   No. 51

Mr. Frelinghuysen of New Jersey
Honoring 100 Years of History

Mr. Speaker, I rise today to honor the Borough of Mendham in Morris County, New Jersey, a vibrant community I am proud to represent! On May 15, 2006 the good citizens of Mendham Borough are celebrating the Borough's Centennial Anniversary.

Mendham Borough, a country village some 6 miles square, was once a stop for stagecoaches traveling on the old Washington Turnpike. The area is hilly, well wooded and its springs and small brooks are feeders for the Passaic and Raritan rivers.

The Borough of Mendham was created out of an urgent need to install a public water distribution system to fight fires and protect the lives and the property of its citizens. This it has done for 100 years, since its establishment as an incorporated municipality on May 15, 1906. Before incorporation, it was part of Mendham Township. The Borough's village center (largely unchanged from the 1800s) serves as the hub of commercial activity for the Mendhams.

Mendham Borough is the site of five Historic American Buildings and a registered National Historic District. The leading landmark building and the Borough's icon is the classic Federalist style Phoenix House, a former genteel and fashionable roadhouse. Most famous amongst its regular guests was General Abner Doubleday, best known as the inventor of baseball. This majestic building, recently restored, serves as the Borough Hall.

Today, Mendham Borough is comprised of modest homes, small estates, and individual retail stores with some remaining open space. Its population exceeds 5,000.

Mr. Speaker, I urge you and my colleagues to join me in congratulating the residents of Mendham Borough on the celebration of 100 years of rich history of one of New Jersey's finest municipalities!

History written into the *Congressional Record* by Representative Rodney Frelinghuysen.

119

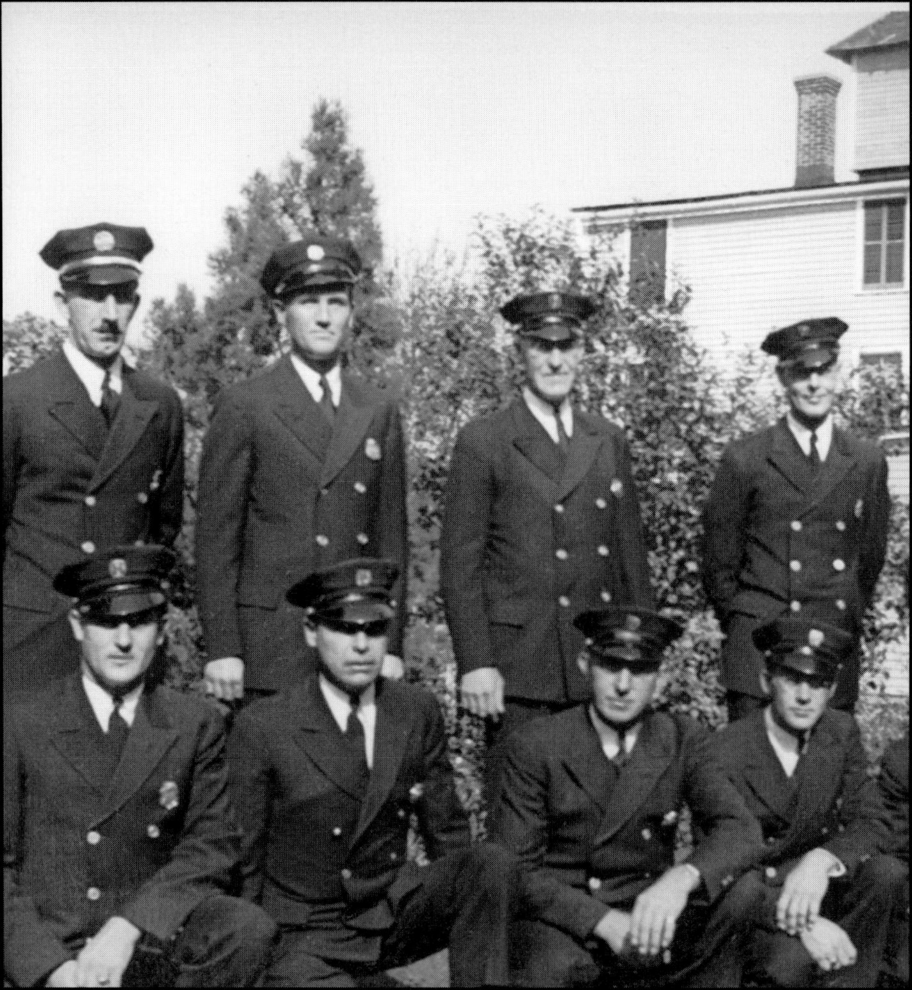

Chapter Seven
Protecting and Serving

*...It started out with neighbors wanting to help neighbors...
Our comrades who have gone before laid the groundwork for us to grow to
what we are today.... As long as we remember, neighbor helping neighbor,
that's what it is all about, we will continue to grow and thrive in the future.*

—Thomas Berenbak
Fire Chief 2004-05
One hundredth anniversary message

Evolution of Emergency Services— Fire and First Aid

While technology, education requirements, and the demands of a growing community have required our emergency services to adapt to varying needs through the years, volunteering one's time in support of one's neighbors has been a common thread, as demonstrated with the inception of the fire department in 1905, first aid squad in 1940, and women's auxiliary in 1950. Volunteer members respond to fire and first aid calls twenty-four hours a day, seven days a week, and are active in many of our community activities. Through the very well documented and preserved history of the fire department, we can trace much of the evolution of our emergency services since 1905.

John Smith consults with a rookie fireman on Fire Prevention Day.
Courtesy of Carolyn Menagh

Creation of the Bucket Brigade

In reporting on the borough's seventy-fifth anniversary, an article in the *Observer Tribune* succinctly described the concern and the need of a town of wooden structures and many farms:

Top left: 1905 fire truck pulled by horses Prince and Brownie. *Courtesy of Mendham Fire Department*

Top right: Reenactment of hose drill with T. Berenbak, W. Menagh Jr., C. Crotsley, K. Betz, J. Egan, J. Eible, D. Ellis, and B. Watkins. *Courtesy of Mendham Fire Department*

Bottom: Mendham Fire Department, 1908. *Courtesy of Mendham Fire Department*

> *For small towns such as the Borough in 1905, a fire in a wooden structure was one of the residents' most haunting fears. Smaller homes could be destroyed in minutes. Larger two or three-story houses with narrow, open stairwells were especially susceptible to fire. Most feared were the mammoth barn fires. Tinder-dry and filled with hay, they literally exploded into unquenchable flames that killed livestock and destroyed equipment.*
>
> —Observer Tribune, May 14, 1981

It was this type of motivation that led a group of men to meet on June 10, 1905, to form a bucket brigade. This was the inception of the Mendham Fire Department. While today's fire department provides our community with a variety of services including fire prevention, fire suppression, and rescue services through the use of advanced equipment and formal training, in 1905, the groundwork was just being established.

On June 20, 1905, the name "Mendham Fire Department" was formally adopted, and officers were elected, with John Hoffman as chief. Sixty-one men became charter members of the department.

At that time, there was no formal annual fundraising or formalized process for obtaining financial support from the town. The group formed a committee to undertake a fundraising effort. Their decision was to hold a dance or ball, and so began a tradition of recognizing the fundraising committee of the fire department as the Ball Committee. The first "ball" raised $264.98 toward the purchase of a horse-drawn vehicle, referred to as a hook and ladder truck, costing $885.

But there was no firehouse in which to store the vehicle. While planning was taking place for a firehouse, in May 1906, John Hoffman built a shed behind his building on Main Street to store the hook and ladder truck until a firehouse was built. The new firehouse, located at 21 West Main Street, was completed in December 1906. Today it is the offices of Weichert Realtors. After the town had purchased, moved, and converted the old Methodist Church, the department moved to East Main Street, where the entrance of today's firehouse sits. In 1980 part of this original building was kept and moved to a new firehouse built on the site of the nursery to the rear. If one looks at the current firehouse from the east side, the original round window can be seen.

While the borough provided for construction of the new firehouse, much of the interior was constructed by volunteer efforts of the firemen at very little cost to the taxpayers. Furniture was purchased with firehouse funds, and several local businesses donated time and supplies to the construction. The women's auxiliary lent a hand with the interior design of the firehouse. The ladies used their funds to purchase several of the curtains, drapes, and kitchen necessities and furnishings.

A short distance from Hoffman's shed, which housed the first hook and ladder truck, but a long way in the development of our emergency services, the existing firehouse is home to the fire department, first aid squad, and women's auxiliary and houses six fire trucks and vehicles and two ambulances.

In 1905 there were no uniforms, but that was quickly rectified when the uniform of the New York Fire Department was adopted, and new uniforms costing $13.50 each were purchased. In August 1907 the department traveled to Hackettstown by train to attend their first parade. They had hired a band with the hopes of winning first place; they didn't. Two years later, they did much better when they employed a drillmaster instead and came back from Plainfield with a prize for the "Best-Looking" uniformed company.

In March 1913 the department was incorporated and changed its name to the Mendham Independent Hook and Ladder Company. After incorporation, the borough council passed a resolution forming a new company to be placed under its jurisdiction. This was the Mendham Hose Company. The purpose was to allow the Borough of Mendham a means of providing support to the fire department. Until this time, the department paid for all maintenance and housing of equipment. The independent company turned over equipment consisting of a hose cart, hose, nozzles, and other necessary equipment, and it became the proving ground for the new men. Certain qualifications had to be met before the men were recommended to the council for election to the hose company. Acceptance to the fire department has continued in the same fashion since 1913.

Top: Today, Prince and Brownie ride on the fire department's ladder 83 truck. *Courtesy of Mendham Fire Department*

Bottom: The Roxiticus Clubhouse fire in 1979 is widely viewed as the worst in Mendham history. The structure was a total loss, and the manager and his wife perished. *Courtesy of Mendham Fire Department*

Members of the fire department display trophy won at Firematics annual event competition among ten towns in 1997: back (l-r) B. Jenkins, R. Cacchio; middle: R. De Nicola, J. Rae, M. Bruin, Joe Eile Jr., M. Orgera, R. Orgera; front: R. Bruin, M. Moro, S. Basko, D. Laurano, Jason Eible, Tom Porter (with trophy). *Courtesy of Mendham Fire Department*

Original car wheel used for sounding alarms stands at the East Main Street entrance to the firehouse. *Courtesy of Mendham Fire Department*

Fire department, 2006—Standing (l-r): Fr. Michael Drury, Drew Gizzi, Tom Porter, Charlie Grebenstein, Bill Crutchlow, Clay Borchard, Mike Landers, Tim Gilligan, Tom Gilligan, Dave Gizzi, Chris Nelson, Craig Bellamy, Dave Chakrin, Kyle Hastings, Mike Kelly, Darren Fitzpatrick, John Deighan, Tom Berenbak, Ben Jenkins, Bill Bergman, Curran Lucke, William Menagh Sr. Seated (l-r): Dave Crotsley, Bob Collins, Mike Bruin, Mike Orgera, Ed Tencza, Rich DeNicola, Robert Raymond Sr., Earl Barnes Jr. *Courtesy of Mendham Fire Department*

FIRE ALARM

CALLS FOR THE BOROUGH OF MENDHAM

In case of Fire call "Mendham Telephone Central" from the nearest telephone; give operator location of fire and the alarm will be sounded from the Hill Top Church bell.

Number of Districts as follows:

No.
- 3 Test at Noon Daily.
- 56 Center of Town.
- 57 Fire House.
- 72 West Main St.
  - Liberty Pole to Dan Sutton's
- 126 East Main St.
  - Liberty Pole to Oak Tree
- 127 Gunther's St.
- 135 Prospect and New Sts.
- 316 Church St.
  - Liberty Pole to Hill Top Church
- 415 Mountain Ave.
  - Liberty Pole to Wise's Corner

In case of fire outside of these districts, call will be Fire House. 3 taps will signify that fire is out.

In 1943 a junior fire department was formed for boys in the seventh and eighth grades of the local school. The boys could help fight grass and wood fires. In 1972 the Junior Fireman Squad, which exists today, was incorporated into the fire department bylaws. When junior members turn eighteen, they are eligible to be sworn in as regular members of the department.

Known as Station 18, Mendham Borough's Fire Department consists of forty-seven active members and thirty-five retired members. Since its charter in 1905, the department has had a total of 444 members. The department makes about 150 fire calls a year. To operate today's technology and keep up with the demands and safety for fighting fires, today's firefighters undergo 151 hours of training.

From Car Wheel to Plectrons

In 1905 department members debated over whether $6 was too much to pay for a car wheel to sound an alarm of fire in the borough. Ultimately, two car wheels were purchased, one being placed by Gunther Garage and the other by the Freeman Building. One of the car wheels stands today on Main Street at the entrance to the firehouse close to its original site.

As technology changed through the years, so did methods of alarm. In January 1913 a system installed in the First Presbyterian church would signal the location of a fire via the number of bells that would ring when discs placed in a clock would make contact with the bell. Big weights were hung in

Left: Fire alarm call signals. *Courtesy of Mendham Fire Department*

Top right: Hose drill, 1909, was conducted to test water pressure. At the time, water pressure was only sufficient to reach halfway up the Hilltop Church steeple. *Courtesy of Mendham Fire Department*

Bottom right: The Tap Mansion fire occurred in 1990 during renovations in which contractors' torches ignited a fire in the rafters. *Courtesy of Mendham Fire Department*

Chapter Seven: Protecting and Serving 125

Left: First ambulance, 1935 Ford woody, donated by William Cordingly. *Courtesy of Mendham First Aid Squad*

Right: Charter members of the First Aid Rescue Squad, established in 1940: Jacob T. Lewis, Director; James Gunther, assistant director; Richard Clark, quartermaster; Charles Moeri, chief; Clinton J. Barnett, secretary-treasurer; Joseph Ammerman; Charles Day; Floyd Garabrant; Orville Garabrant; Cyrill Lounsbury; Francis B. Prior; William Menagh Sr. *Courtesy of Mendham Fire Department*

the church steeple, and two men were needed to operate the system. The first siren was ordered in March 1922 and used in the borough until 1955. Phone calls from the alarm center to the firehouse would provide the location of the call. In 1972 the fire department asked the borough council to look into a new alert system that used plectrons to alert volunteers as to the location and nature of the call, thus saving valuable time. Today all members of our fire department and first aid squad wear a plectron beeper activated by radio signals issued by centralized dispatchers, who receive 911 calls. The signals have a range of thirty miles.

A dedicated person who should not be forgotten is Helen Rae. Rae served as the Mendham Borough around-the-clock fire alarm operator for sixteen years. She sounded the alarm for fires, civil defense, and first aid calls. Her quiet, reassuring voice was always a comfort to anyone in trouble or with a problem. The auxiliary button for the alarm was located at Robinson's Drug Shop, but was very seldom used, as Rae was always on the job.

Birth and Evolution of the First Aid Squad

In 1940 the fire department held a discussion centered on forming a first aid squad. Twelve men indicated that they would be willing to take the standard first aid course. An E&J resuscitator was purchased, and Dr. F. Clyde Bowers was made medical advisor to the squad. The squad became the Mendham First Aid Rescue Squad and would serve both Mendham Borough and Mendham Township until 1969, when the township squad was formed.

William Cordingley donated the first ambulance to the squad. It was a 1935 Ford station wagon, and a good deal of work was done on it—leveling the floor, building a rack for the resuscitator and a compartment for splints and other equipment. Cordingley assumed all the expense. The squad's first new ambulance was a Cadillac purchased in 1944 through donations obtained by members. This ambulance was not replaced until it was ten years old. Today Mendham Borough has two ambulances fully equipped with stretchers, radios, defibrillators, oxygen, and equipment tailored to both the needs of adults and children.

Chiefs of the Mendham Fire Department

J. M. Hoffman	1905–1907	H. Traudt	1962–1963
F. Freeman	1908	R. Sanderson	1964–1965
F. R. Guerin	1909–1910	J. O'Keefe	1966–1967
C. H. Day	1911–1915	R. Snedaker	1968–1969
F. Freeman	1916–1918	W. Shank	1970–1971
F. Groendyke	1919–1920	John Grassi	1972–1973
L. Robinson	1921–1922	E. Barnes	1974–1975
F. R. Guerin	1923–1924	C. Watkins	1976–1977
G. Delp	1925–1926	D. Smith	1978–1979
C. M. Day	1927–1928	E. Tully	1980–1981
F. Woodruff	1929	C. D. Crotsley	1982–1983
G. L. Day	1930–1931	J. Eible Sr.	1984
G. Thompson	1932–1933	C. Watkins	1985
V. Garabrant	1934–1935	E. Finlay	1986–1987
W. Rockafeller	1936–1937	T. Berenbak	1988–1989
J. Sullivan	1938–1939	J. Hoffman	1990–1991
C. Moeri Jr.	1940–1941	T. Porter	1992–1993
E. Watkins	1942–1943	F. Scharfenberg	1994–1995
C. Guerin	1944–1945	T. Berenbak	1995
W. Menagh	1946–1947	T. Porter	1996
J. Gunther	1948–1949	R. Raymond	1996–1997
R. J. Clark	1950–1951	W. Menagh Jr.	1998–1999
J. T. Lewis	1952–1953	J. Smith	2000–2001
H. Dean	1954–1955	J. Eible Jr.	2002–2003
P. Parrillo	1956–1957	T. Berenbak	2004–2005
J. Dormer	1958–1959	M. Orgera	2006–Present
F. Crammer	1960–1961		

The first patient call was on July 4, 1940—a fireworks operator with first-degree burns. From its inception, the squad provided mutual aid support to other communities where and when they were needed. They volunteered their time for an explosion at the Hercules powder plant and worked at Dover General Hospital, helping with the incoming injured. In 1940 and 1941, they provided demonstrations as far as Whippany and Cedar Knolls to generate support for first aid in the Morristown Red Cross area. On July 26, 1952, the Mendham First Aid Squad assisted other squads in Morris County in moving patients from old Memorial Hospital to the new hospital. Within one hour and fifty-five minutes, they moved sixty-three patients a distance of three and a half miles.

By 1950 the Mendham First Aid Rescue Squad had responded to ninety calls a year. By 1967, when calls had reached close to 180, the squad felt the area they were covering was too large—there were too many calls and too little manpower. They appealed to Mendham Township, which formed its own squad in 1969. Through the years, members of both squads have enjoyed a strong bond of mutual support during times when multiple ambulances are required. Many members belong to both squads and respond in either town.

In recent years, Mendham Borough's first aid members have responded to between four hundred and five hundred calls a year.

In January 2004 change once again took place. The first aid squad, feeling the need to govern itself and address the needs of advanced training and financing, became an independent organization. It continues to support the fire department by responding to all fire calls, assisting with potential patients, and conducting rehab for the firefighters.

Through the years, the squad has also seen its evolution from a group of twelve men who initially started the squad to a group of both men and women. In 1997 the Mendham First Aid Squad named its first woman captain. This is a long way from a controversy in the 1970s in which a local woman filed a civil rights action against the fire department as she did not want to become a firefighter before she would be eligible for the first aid squad. For many years, firemen exclusively comprised the first aid squad.

Firefighters and police officers are now cross-trained as emergency medical technicians. Other members are of varying ages and genders and from all walks of life—retired, working, and students.

In 1940, when members joined the first aid squad, they were responsible for obtaining training in basic first aid offered by the American Red Cross. Today the multi-tier first aid response system provides three levels of care: local basic life services, paramedic support, and hospital care. The training requirements of the first aid squad have significantly increased. Thirty-five of the forty members of today's squad are EMTs who have more than 120 hours of training, including CPR and the use of defibrillators. Continuing-education credits of at least twenty-four hours must be earned over three years to maintain EMT certification.

Top: Rescue workers prepare for boarding a North Star helicopter at West Field. *Courtesy of Carolyn Menagh*

Bottom: Members of the Women's Auxiliary celebrate the fire department's one hundredth anniversary at Roxiticus Golf Club: (l-r) Chris Day, Carolyn Menagh, Mary Oppel, Evelyn Thompson, Mary Swanson, Julie Kenny. *Courtesy of Mendham Fire Department*

Women's Auxiliary

In 1950 the Women's Auxiliary of the Mendham Fire Department held its first meeting. It had twenty-eight members. The auxiliary supports, encourages, and supplements the firefighters of the Mendham Fire Department in their service to the community. Membership in the auxiliary consists of wives, mothers, daughters, sisters, and widows of active and associate members of the department.

Through the years, the women's auxiliary has taken a very active role in fundraising support for the fire department. It has hosted activities such as fun nights, bake sales, tricky trays, casino nights, and spaghetti or fish and chips dinners to raise money. Through the years, they and many more have purchased floor covering and flags for the firehouse, and two-way radio equipment and a resuscitator for the first aid squad. In times of emergency, the auxiliary has been awakened to help provide food and beverages for our fire department and its mutual aid partners.

First Aid Rescue Squad Directors/Captains

Jacob Lewis	1940–1942	Joseph Murphy	1976–1977
C. Barnettt	1943–1945	Edward Finlay	1978–1979
Richard Clark	1946–1947	Craig Bellamy	1980
Phillip Parrillo Sr.	1948–1949	Thomas Berenbak	1981
John Moeri	1950–1951	Kenneth Betz	1982–1983
Lloyd Belton	1952–1953	Robert Bretzger Sr.	1984–1985
Harold Traudt	1954–1955	Frank Scharfenberg	1986–1987
Richard Finlay	1956–1957	William Menagh Jr.	1988–1989
Robert Snedaker	1958–1959	Edward Finlay	1990
John Grassi	1960–1961	Thomas Berenbak	1991
William Menagh Sr.	1962–1963	Joseph Eible Jr.	1992–1993
Arthus Thompson	1964–1965	Calvin DePew	1994–1996
Donald Smith	1966–1967	Peggy Berenbak	1997–1999
William Conover	1968–1969	Jason DePew	2000–2001
C. David Crotsley	1970–1971	David Murphy	2001–2003
Richard Apgar	1972-1973	Barbara Nelson	2004–Present
Robert Phillips	1974–1975	(now Mendham First Aid Squad)	

Mendham First Aid Squad, 2005. (L-r) seated: Paula Oswald, David Murphy, Barbara Nelson, Lauren Houdlich—(l-r) standing: Jay Alderton, Lelia Garcia, Tim Gilligan, Jim Hendren, Tom Gilligan, Noreen Staples, Bob Raymond, Sgt. Rich Morales, Fr. Mike Drury, Diana Callahan, Bill Shaw, Peggy Berenbak, Chris Nelson, Trish Cleary, Marleen Russell, Vincent Reilly, Jim Cillo, Sgt. Pat McNichol, Tom Berenbak. *Courtesy of Mendham First Aid Squad*

Chapter Seven: Protecting and Serving

Supporting Community Events

Traditionally, the fire department held an annual Halloween Party for the children of the town. The party was held until 1966, when the number of children was getting too large to handle. It had grown to six hundred. They also implemented TOT finders in 1959, in which decals were purchased and placed on windows of homes where children and/or invalids lived.

In 1960 Fire Prevention Week began. The hope was that if school children were given an interesting program, they would take it home to their parents. Also, if you live on the northern side of town, you are also familiar with the sirens of the trucks on Labor Day as the department provides fire truck rides from Borough Park. What you might not know is that the proceeds from the rides are donated to the New Jersey Burn Victims Foundation.

Mendham First Aid Squad is active in community education. They have given presentations to Boy/Girl Scouts and Cub Scouts/Brownies as well as our senior citizens. They have distributed the File of Life to many of our residents, helping them have medications and medical history available in advance of a potential first aid call. They also give support to Mendham High School on such activities as football games, the humanities festival, and graduation. The squad is also active in Labor Day activities.

Mutual Aid with Our Mendham Neighbors

Mendham fire and first aid work closely through mutual aid with our Mendham Township and Bernardsville neighbors. During fires, accidents, or multiple calls at the same time, neighbors call on all to help each other. Through the years, Mendham Borough has called on their mutual aid neighbors when major fires struck at Roxiticus Golf Club, the Tap Mansion, and Gunther Automotive.

The Disappearance of Local Boundaries

Given the changing society, recent terrorist events, and natural disasters, new training has been mandated for firefighters and first aiders. Today's members are not only trained as firefighters and EMTs, but also receive training on hazardous materials awareness, weapons of mass destruction, incident command, and search and rescue. No longer are our emergency services operating just in their own municipality with residents and visitors, but must also be aware of the likelihood that they may be called upon to respond to major incidents.

Top: Members of the First Aid Squad display a plaque presented by the Port Authority in appreciation of their response on 9/11/2001: Tom Berenbak, Paula Oswald, David Murphy, James Hendren. *Photo by Diana Callahan*

Middle: First-aiders Dave Murphy and Barbara Nelson join the Fire Department in the rescue of an "extended family member" at the mud hole. *Mendham Borough archives*

Bottom: Mendham firemen waiting to help on September 11, 2001. *Courtesy of Carolyn Menagh*

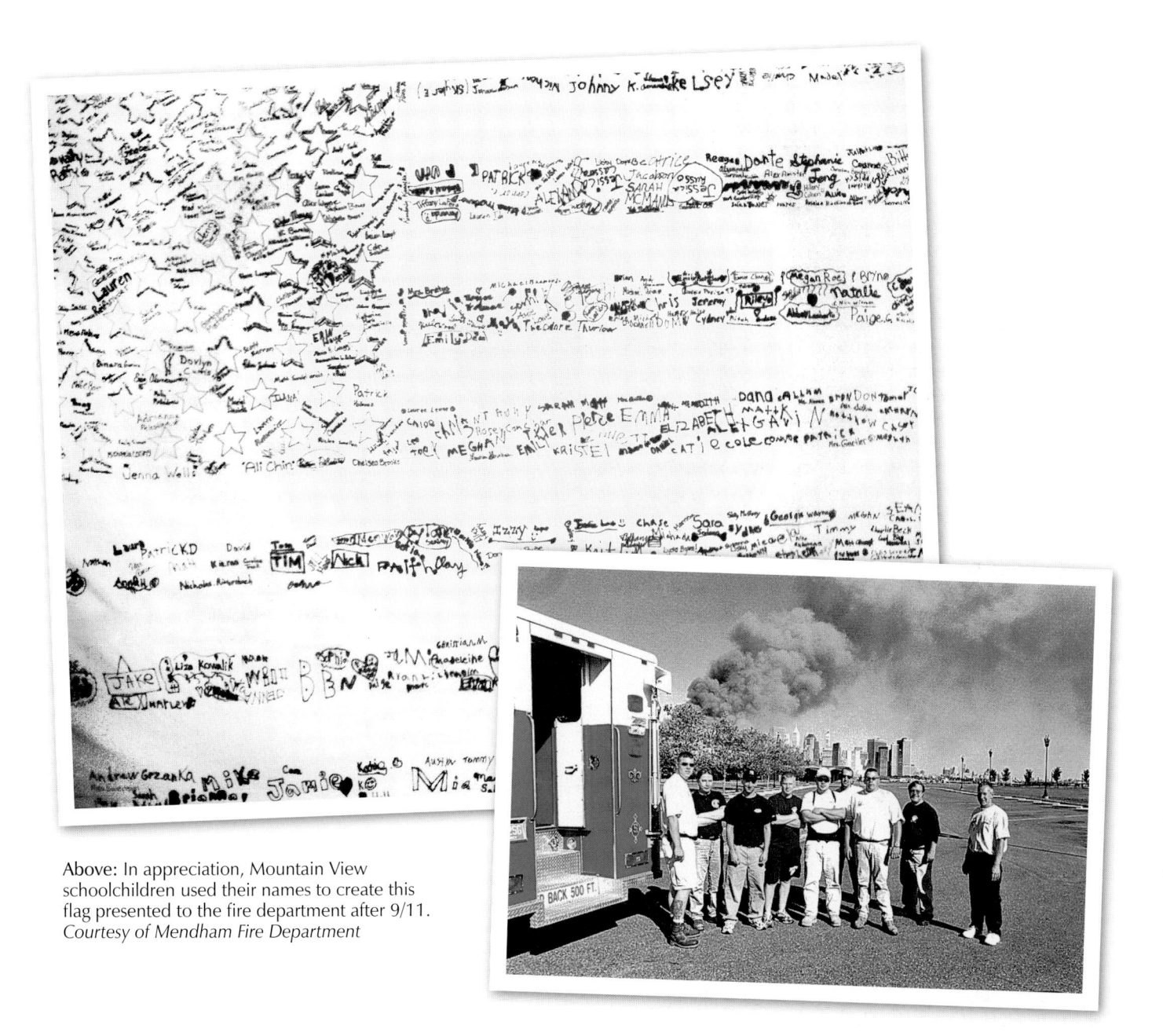

Above: In appreciation, Mountain View schoolchildren used their names to create this flag presented to the fire department after 9/11. *Courtesy of Mendham Fire Department*

Above: Responding on 9/11/2001. (L-r) William Pugsley Jr., Peter Taylor, Bruce LaFera, Chris Nelson, Ed Tencza, Paul Nelson, Bill Taquinto, Tom Berenbak, Bill Menagh Jr. Not pictured: John Smith. *Courtesy of John Smith and Carolyn Menagh*

September 11, 2001, remains forever embedded in the minds of all Americans. The Mendham Fire Department and First Aid Rescue Squad were called into service by New Jersey to assist with rescue and triage. The department responded by 11:30 a.m., reporting to Liberty State Park to await barges that were to bring injured survivors from the scene. They were sent home at 10:30 p.m. as there were no injured survivors to be triaged. The first aid squad was sent into New York on subsequent days to assist in first aid response. Other fire and first aid squad members stayed in Mendham to support our residents feeling the pain of that difficult time.

From Then until Always

While large fires and incidents gain the most attention, events such as the unpublished fire that was put down before it had a chance to expand, the person rescued from entrapment, the new baby born en route to the hospital, and the breath brought back are the motivation and the rewards for our fire and first aid volunteers.

Chapter Seven: Protecting and Serving

Mendham Borough Police Department

They want to get to know you to help you out rather than punish you. It took a while to get used to that.

—Diana Callahan on moving to Mendham

The "Flintstone Era"

At the incorporation of the borough in 1906, the small municipality had no full-time officers, but was instead served by part-time "marshals" appointed annually by the mayor and council. They took care of minor complaints, often resolving the incidents or altercations at the scene. (New Jersey state troopers were called in for more serious crimes.) If not resolved at the scene, the involved parties would be brought before the local judge (a lay person magistrate) for a hearing. For many years, Judge Hankinson, a local painter, served as magistrate, and hearings took place at his home, but in the 1950s J. Branton Wallace became the first attorney appointed as magistrate.

Early marshals included Chiefs John Tiger, Mike Cacchio, Phil Parrillo, Ed Hill, and Fred Koenik. Harold Brill served the borough simultaneously as chief marshal and road and water department foreman. Around 1948 Chief Brill became the first full-time marshal; as the borough did not provide a vehicle, he patrolled in his Plymouth convertible squad car. There is no record of his receiving a mileage allowance.

Police calls were routed to Mrs. Rae at the Phoenix House or to Mrs. Brill at her home. Without radios or car phones, Chief Brill had to periodically check in to get his calls. At the time, there was a blinker light mounted on the broken flagpole in the center of Route 24 at the Phoenix House, and atop the blinker was placed a small white light that Mrs. Brill could switch on from her home. If the chief was directing traffic and saw the light, he knew he had to phone home. Later, when the pole was removed and the traffic blinker light was suspended high over the center of the intersection, an outside phone bell was installed at police headquarters, located in the basement of the Phoenix House. When Mrs. Rae or Mrs. Brill needed to contact the chief, they rang the bell, and he would leave traffic duty to answer the phone. To improve response time, a call box extension was later installed on the public phone box in the front of Robinson's Drug Store.

Chief Brill resigned in 1954, and the title changed when Walter Smith, a deputy marshal, became the first chief of police, beginning the transition from the "Flintstone Era" to a modern force. He was the first borough officer to attend the Municipal Police Training Course at the New Jersey State Police Academy in Sea Girt. During his short tenure, the borough purchased its first

Left: Jim Cillo, well before being named chief. *Mendham Borough Police Department*

Right: Anthony Cillo with Phil Parrillo Sr., one of the first marshals in town. *Courtesy of Honey Belton*

police car, a radio-equipped Ford. Although the chief could call for backup from other forces, the officers still had no portable radios and, as a result, had to sign out and call in with a phone number whenever they left their vehicle.

In 1957 Chief Smith resigned, and Earl Moore, a sergeant in Roxbury, was hired. He remained the only full-time officer. Chief Moore worked the day shift Monday through Saturday, and on evenings and Sundays special officers did a little patrolling but mostly took emergency calls at their homes. On March 1, 1959, the force expanded to two officers and after training at Sea Girt, Jim Cillo became the first borough patrolman.

Transition

The 1950s and '60s may not sound like a long time ago, but retired chief Cillo's recollections paint a picture that may surprise many of us:

> We would think nothing of seeing hunters like Tim Pierson walking up Lake Road with a shotgun to hunt on what is now the West Field soccer field, Townsend Road, and St. John's hill off Hilltop Road. Hunters like Jerry Havas would hunt deer in the Florie Farm and Pitney Farm woods as well as along Patriot's Path in areas that now comprise the shopping center, Phoenix, Knollwood, Forrest, and Dean Roads, as well as what now belongs to Holly Manor and the Commons.
>
> "In 1959 and the early '60, it was not uncommon to go down Pitney Road in back of Joe Moro's garage, Louie Moro's and my cousin, Pete Cillo's, houses to round up Pitney Farm cows that had broken through the fence, where Holly Manor and the Commons are now. There were calls on Hilltop Road at Duck Pond Farm (just below Sisters of Christian Charity) when Mrs. Granger's very large pigs would break the fence and stampede toward the Sisters. We would call John Diegan Sr., and we with our nightsticks, John with corn and a rake, and some of the nuns swinging brooms, would round up the pigs. As the pigs got bigger, there were more breaks, but, fortunately Mrs. Granger eventually got rid of them.
>
> "On other calls we would be chasing loose horses in Joe Backer's cornfield (now Quimby Lane), and on one call a horse was loose in a field of eight-foot-tall corn—he was a big horse. I had to do something, so I went into the field, and a half-hour of searching, it occurred to me how afraid of horses I was. A rapid return was made back to the patrol car; thank God I hadn't found the horse which had returned to the barn on its own. I bluffed my way out of that one.

Left: The police force lines up for a charity game at Mendham High, 1970s. (L-r) Werner Ablessmeier, Dave Ausicker, George Vanderbush, second from right, Jim Cillo. For many years, George Vanderbush coached the high school Girls JV Team and assisted in the successful varsity program. *Mendham Borough Police Department*

Right: 1997 recipients of police scholarships. More than $207,000 has been awarded. Far left, Chief Vanderbush (Ret.); in rear, Capt. Gaffney (Ret.); on right, Chief Patricia Cameron (Ret.). *Mendham Borough Police Department*

> WHAT NOW STANDS IN THE PLACE OF JOE'S SNACK BAR, AND FOR WHAT WAS JOE'S KNOWN?
>
> ANSWER: SOMERSET HILLS BANK. NOT THE FOOD.

Chapter Seven: Protecting and Serving

From One Shot…

Not all canines were as friendly as Bill Boggis'. There was a stray dog in a little shack behind Joe's Snack Bar and Sammy's Auto Body. Old "Joe" (I never knew his last name) lived in the shack and would walk down to the brook every spring to get his bath—and maybe one or two more in the summer and fall. This was not the case with his dog, its fur matted and dirty, and with a nasty disposition. The dog started getting more nasty than normal, and Sammy DeFillips and Joe Giglio became concerned as the dog began giving their customers and them a hard time. They didn't have the heart to go to old Joe, and I had the misfortune of being on duty this particular Sunday. Old Joe was gone, perhaps taking a bath, and I was told something was wrong with the dog, as he had become nasty and threatening to everyone in the area.

Yours truly responded and was confronted by the dog, which charged at me barking and showing its teeth. He was coming at me fast and furious, and I knew I had to be quick. I drew my .38-caliber revolver and pegged a shot at the dog, which abruptly stopped and ran into a pile of brush and tree branches. I knew I missed the dog for there was no blood, he wasn't limping but running fast— and I had observed the shot hitting quite a ways behind him. Of course, I didn't tell anyone that. However, I had to poke through the brush pile, and although he made nary a sound, I spotted him in the middle of the large heap. The trusty revolver was drawn again, careful aim was taken, a shot fired, the dog didn't move, there was no sound, so I pointed the revolver up, blew the smoke away, and holstered my weapon. The onlookers were convinced the job was done, and I went back to patrolling. The next day when I reported to work, Chief Moore laughed and began calling me "one shot." Well One Shot, the news is that the dog walked back to the house, was easily rounded up by the chief (he had a way with dogs), and was taken to the vet. I lived with "One Shot'" for quite a while.

—Chief Jimmy Cillo

Joe's Snack Bar, site of the One Shot Episode. *Courtesy of Don Preziosi*

The beginning of change may have been initiated by the Bank Robbery of 1961:

The Great Bank Robbery

Life Magazine's January 5, 1962, edition contained a two-page "Special Report" on the robbery of Morris County Savings Bank's Mendham office, titled "The Great but Very, Very Late Bank Robbery." The article was written as one might a light comedy, not quite a farce, and not everyone in Mendham considered it fully complimentary. But stripping away the author's efforts at humor, one can conclude that Mendham, a town of twenty-seven hundred in the early 1960s, and its police force played it perfectly. Bottom line: the two robbers took nearly two years to finally decide to commit the heist, and being strangers in town, by that time not only the police force but nearly everyone else in the borough knew and was prepared for what was coming. Chief Moore saw the robbers casing the bank on their first visit in March 1960. He spoke to them on their second. An anonymous tip was received, license plates were run, and the name of one of the pair, William Redic, was identified. Chief Moore had a folder—"Planned Robbery of Mendham Bank"—that he continually updated—Redic and his partner, Robert Grogan, are spotted in town; Redic was in the ice cream parlor, Redic was here, there . . . . In December, Redic finally entered the bank, was identified by the manager, and while Moore watched from across the street, Murph Rae called the manager, Herb Miller, from the butcher shop to let him know the getaway the car was outside. The robbers inquired about getting a mortgage. No robbery. Everything was on hold. Redic asked about Friday night late hours. Friday night, the chief waited in the butcher shop with Officer Jim Cillo and special officer Eddie Fagan. The robbers came, the robbers left. Six more months passed. Redic and Grogan showed up again— half the town identifies them. Redic drops into Fagan's grocery store, buys butts, asks for a job—no deal. Finally, the day of reckoning. Moore is waiting, Cillo is on a ladder, painting St. Joseph's Church—his pistol at arm's reach in the church gutter— Murph Rae calls the station again; phone's busy, so he asks customer Mary Cacchio to deliver a note wrapped in a bag of bones to police headquarters and alert Moore. The robbers go into the bank and emerge with $10,678, only to meet Chief Moore (who has had to wend his way through the Garden Club meeting at the Phoenix House to reach the curb), carbine in hand, Officer Cillo, gun now out of the rain gutter, officer Geraghty and two special officers drafted for the occasion. The arrest is made.

A serious, potentially very dangerous event identified on the initial visit of a stranger and finally thwarted almost two years later.

Expansion

In 1965 the force expanded from a two-man department to five men; the position of sergeant was created, and Jim Cillo moved into that slot. Joe Collins, Bob Brunisholz, and Ken Nelson were appointed patrolmen, but they covered only the day and evening shifts. At midnight the last shift took the patrol car home to respond to any emergency calls during the unmanned shift.

However, in 1968 there was a safe burglary at Foodtown (now Kings) in the Village Shopping Center, and in 1969 a car was stolen from Freeman (now Maplecrest) Ford. In Foodtown the suspects (never apprehended) drilled through the roof, climbed down, and broke open the safe. In Freeman Ford

Left: The 2006 Borough Police Force. Back row: Ptl. Brian Hostler, Sgt. Patrick McNichol, Ptl. Christopher Gobbi, Sgt. John Camoia, Det. Christopher Hopf, Ptl. Lee Barnes, Chief John Taylor. First Row: Sgt. Rich Morales, Sgt. Pat Libertino, Ptl. Joe Parrillo, Ptl. Joe Kennedy, Ptl. Joe Farry.

Right: 2006 Chief John "J. T." Taylor.

they simply broke in, took the keys to a new vehicle, and fled. As both crimes occurred during the unmanned midnight shift, it was deemed necessary to once again expand the department, and in 1970 the staff increased to nine officers with around-the-clock patrols.

With the opening of West Morris Mendham High School in the borough, the department was increased to eleven officers, and in March 1978, Chief Moore retired and Lieutenant Cillo took over. The department was increased to twelve, the detective bureau was enlarged, and the D.A.R.E. drug prevention program in the schools was initiated.

Although crime may not have been rampant, it was not totally unknown. An armed robbery attempt at Sorrento's Pizzeria on East Main was thwarted when the police received a tip in advance. Later, Detective Gary Gaffney was credited with apprehending the suspects in a cigarette truck heist that took place in Bernardsville. "The Bernardsville PD chased the subjects and lost them in one of the parking lots. They put an alarm out and Gaffney spotted the suspects car parked next to the Sandrellen estate on Hilltop Road. Their clothing during the job and some of the loot was spotted in plain view inside the car. This was not surprising. Having clearly flunked 'Prior Planning for a Heist,' the suspects had run out of gas, walked to Gunther's station to fill a gas container, and were apprehended while walking back to the car."

"Gas and Hilltop Road was seemingly a common theme. In another incident, the police were called when a motorist ran out of gas. His gauge wasn't working. He looked for a flashlight in the car but couldn't find one, so he got out of the car and took off the gas cap to look in and see if there was any gas. Unable to see, he took out his matches and lit one to illuminate the tank. Fortunately, he survived the ensuing explosion, leaving the scene with a 'sunburned' face, a very high forehead, and minus his eyebrows."

In 1982, Chief Cillo and Lt. George Vanderbush explored the idea of having a police chaplain available to act as a confidant in police matters, as well as to tend to the spiritual needs of the department and community. Father Michael J. Drury, an associate pastor of St. Joseph's, was approached. Father Mike accepted the role and has never looked back. His role has expanded to serving in the same capacity for the fire department and first aid squad as well as for other communities, and as chaplain, he has not only guided emergency services personnel through difficult and tragic events, but has also earned sufficient

Top: Police secretaries Penny Andrus and Jean Haverkost. *Mendham Borough Police Department*

Middle: Retired Chief Jim Cillo, an EMS volunteer, and retired Capt. Gaffney, a Father Mike Drury volunteer police clown-a-round, await the start of the Labor Day Parade. *Courtesy of Diana Callahan*

Bottom: Officer Joe Farry assists the Stanton family during the Fishing Derby as Officer Joe Kennedy enjoys his coffee.

...to Six Shots

Chief Taylor spent eight years with the Essex County police and was Jim Cillo's last hire. It is rumored he was the cause of Cillo's retirement—perhaps a reminder of days past. As "J. T." notes:

I was not good with shooting injured animals. The idea was to shoot the animal once and put it out of its misery. It usually took me six or seven shots to complete the job. One day I got a call for a sick or injured animal on Hardscrabble Road. I found the raccoon lying on its back on the storm water grate. I guess the word got out that Taylor was a bad shot, and if he were the one to put you out of your misery, then you were in big trouble. I could have sworn that when I approached the raccoon, he made eye contact and recognized me. As I drew my weapon, he used every bit of remaining energy to roll over and down the sewer system to escape— better suicide than facing "six-shot" Taylor.

—J. T. Taylor

respect to be asked to preside at any number of marriages, baptisms, and funerals.

Chief Cillo retired on December 31, 1991, and Lt. Vanderbush took over. Chief Vanderbush, highly organized and a budget-conscious administrator, as well as the consummate police officer, ran a ten-man department and still had time to reach out to the community. He initiated the Police Scholarship Fund, which annually awards scholarships to deserving high school seniors from the borough. More than $207,000 has been awarded to deserving students. He also strongly supported the D.A.R.E. program and was instrumental in establishing a law course taught at Mendham High. Less well known were the many instances of personal assistance the chief gave anonymously to needy residents. So organized was the department that for a time, Chief Vanderbush took over the position of borough administrator and police chief. During this period, department members began training as emergency medical technicians, and they now are able to supplement the Mendham First Aid Squad on emergency calls. Not insignificant has been the contribution to the department by individuals of defibrillators, which have been used to save lives on a number of occasions.

Chief Vanderbush retired in June 2000, and Patricia Cameron took over as the borough's first woman police chief. A strong D.A.R.E. advocate, Chief Cameron started the bike patrol and also had computerized license and warrant checks installed in all police motor vehicles.

After her retirement on January 1, 2006, John "J. T." Taylor stepped into the position of chief of police, and the department seems to have come full circle.

Whether the call is for two loose dogs, a senior in need, or a felony in progress, the borough police department continues to serve and protect, as well as to provide community service.

Sgt. Rich Morales "handcuffs" police secretary Eleanor Sacco to the pole. When the station was located in the basement of the Phoenix House, the pole served as Mendham's only "jail."

Chapter Seven: Protecting and Serving 137

Top left: Bob Snedaker (front, in bow tie) with the 1973 DPW crew. (L-r) Dave Crotsley, Cal Hoffman, Tom Porter, Dick Apgar, Donald Smith, Walter Mosher, Diney LeMonier, Craig Bellamy, Joe Lounsbury, Stanton Bockoven. Front right: Dick Sanderson. *Courtesy of Dave Crotsley*

Top right: Anthony Cillo in front of Robinson's Drug Store. He reputedly dug most of the original water system by hand. *Courtesy of Pete Cillo*

Bottom: The old reservoir and Mendham Borough Water Works. *Mendham*

Department of Public Works

What he did, he did for the Borough of Mendham.
—Dave Crotsley about Bob Snedaker

Charged with the duties of caring for the borough's roads, water, sewers, and parks, the Department of Public Works (DPW) has played a large and increasingly important role in Mendham's controlled growth. Following the formation of an incorporated borough in 1906, the citizens still needed to ratify the construction of a new water system. The original water system was not without controversy, and in a special vote in 1907, the construction of the system passed by only sixteen votes.

The system was built in 1910 at a cost of $40,000, and Frederick V. Pitney owned the water rights. Through the persuasive efforts of Leo Robinson, Pitney deeded them to the borough. He subsequently obtained the position as

Prank or Protest?

Whether prank or protest, in 1915 a $100 reward was offered for the arrest and conviction of the parties who shut the gates and turned the valves, causing the reservoir to empty.

engineer and surveyor for the job, and Robinson became water superintendent. He led a department of two, Dominick Mauro and Anthony "Tony" Cillo, who dug virtually all the connections by hand. Beginning with buildings in the center of town, landowners gradually moved away from their wells and connected to town water. No longer did the town need to count on the springs, cisterns, and hand pumps previously in place.

In 1922 the Combs Hollow Reservoir replaced an original small reservoir, but by the 1940s an increasing population put sufficient pressure on the system to the extent that residents in the southern portion of town often went without water. To remedy the situation, a quarter-million-gallon water tank was built on property off the Bernardsville Road.

One might argue that the modern era for DPW began with the hiring of the first of two individuals, both longtime residents, who guided the borough through its most important decades of expansion. In 1953 Robert Snedaker was named to the posts of water superintendent and borough foreman. Within a few years, a spreading populace looking for just such a place discovered a sleepy, secure, and self-sufficient borough, and as farms were sold and development after development brought greater needs, "Sned" was the man in charge. In 1972 Sned eventually became the first borough administrator, served as a councilman, fire chief, and first aid director, and sat on the Planning Board; and until his death on April 16, 2004, he was the borough's elder

Replacing the evergreen in front of the Phoenix House, 1996. The tree was subsequently cut down in the dead of night, and the culprits were never apprehended, but smart money rides on the initials C. R. and J. S. *Courtesy of Dave Crotsley*

The 1980 DPW staff. Back (l-r): Bobby Walker, unknown, Bill Conover, George Hoagland, Bob Allain, unknown, unknown, Gerry Greco, Dave Crotsley. Front: Walter Mosher, Donald Smith, unknown, Tom Porter, Stephen Thompson, Stanton Bockoven. *Courtesy of Dave Crotsley*

Chapter Seven: Protecting and Serving   139

statesman, advisor, and consultant. His portrait sits in the Phoenix House in a room named in his honor.

In 1968 the borough hired another individual upon whom it would rely for the next thirty-four years. When Bob Snedaker ascended to the newly formed position of borough administrator, Charles "Dave" Crotsley was promoted to superintendent of public works, and for thirty challenging years oversaw the roads, parks, sewers, and water (the water department was sold to the American Water Company in 1991).

Both possessing strong personalities, Crotsley and Snedaker were charged with providing essential services for a borough now exploding with growth, but they worked together because they shared a common goal. As Dave Crotsley explained: "What he (Snedaker) did, he did for the people of Mendham; I learned that from him."

In the late sixties, the DPW crew was an army of six: Sned, Crotsley, Stanton Bockoven, Walt Mosher, Denny LeMonier, and Phil Parrillo Jr. When Crotsley was later asked how the job was done with such a limited staff, the answer was simple and straightforward: "There weren't any roads." It didn't last for long. Deerfield, Bockoven, Gunter, and the Maple Avenue extension used up farmland like falling dominoes. When Mountain View School was built, a contingent of citizens encouraged the town council to purchase the land between the school and Mountain Valley Pool for recreation. In retrospect, it sounds like a good idea, but the offer made to owner Pietro Clementi was well below market. The land was sold to a developer, and the Florie Farm development was built. It was followed closely by Tempe Wick, and suddenly there seemed to be an exponential increase in the miles of roads to be maintained.

During heavy snowstorms, there was no problem getting the crew on site—they all lived in town and could walk. But that's when the fun began. Salt was trucked in on a trailer—one hundred-pound bags to be unloaded and stacked by hand. When needed, the salt and the lawn rotary spreader were loaded on the back of a truck and salt was cranked out by hand.

The entire DPW fleet consisted of two GMC plow trucks and two pickups. A 1940s-vintage grader, needed for the dirt roads, doubled as a snowplow. On heavy snow days, Sam Bockoven could be seen driving through the biting frigid winds of the Deerfield development in the open-cab grader for hours at a time. And when the Phoenix House and Bowers Building staff needed office furniture, you didn't call the decorator and custom order—not when for $5 a desk, chair, or cabinet, you could send the DPW trucks to Sea Girt for army surplus.

As Superintendent Crotsley learned, the job was not simply plowing snow and cutting grass. It took practical knowledge, an ability to improvise, and strong leadership to guide the borough through these times. When the Day Camp arts and crafts director fell through a rotten floor at the "Critter

Top: Phil Parrillo regularly used his jeep to plow the snow off Mountain Valley Pool. This time the jeep ended up submerged and had to be pulled out by a bulldozer, February 1966. *Courtesy of Honey Belton*

Bottom: Dave Crotsley apparently was vacationing in February 1966. On December 21, 1996, Superintendent Crotsley took his jeep out on Mountain Valley Pool to be certain the ice was strong enough for skating; it was not. *Courtesy of Dave Crotsley*

DPW gets ready for traffic control during the Centennial Celebration bike races up Mountain Avenue: (l-r) Robert Orgera, Anna Ravo, Michael Orgera, Darren Thau, Dave Labato, Mike DeFelice, Johnathon Greenemeier.

After plowing all night, the 2006 fleet is parked at the shopping center while the crews get coffee and breakfast, only to continue through most of the next day.

Shack," Crotsley provided damage control; while protesting the removal of a tree on Main Street, a housewife chained herself to the tree, and the first call went to Crotsley; when the park laborer falls asleep at the wheel of his lawn tractor, and removes himself from it by virtue of a low-hanging branch, Crotsley is called in to reload and retrain; and when year-end budgets are strapped and the town needs emergency funds, don't call the finance chairman—have Crotsley search his budget.

Having dealt tangentially with the superintendent and being somewhat intimidated by the no-nonsense personality and reputation of the man who "knows everything," a freshman councilman finds himself in a position of need. Soccer balls are routinely bouncing from West Field into the traffic on Route 24. Knowing that budgeted funds are not available, but finding the nerve to ask "Crotsley" for assistance, a call is made. The request is accepted with no audible proof of commitment, yet less than twenty-four hours later, a post and rail fence, with screening attached, has been erected and a safety issue has been addressed—simply because it's for the people of Mendham.

Chapter Seven: Protecting and Serving

World War I—David Whitehead, Dave O'Keefe, and Albert S. Gray. In back, Walter Kramer. *Courtesy of Gloria Gray*

Marie Cillo Pennimpede, mess sergeant, U.S. Army, WAC, World War II. *Courtesy of Marie Cillo Pennimpede*

Anthony B. Cillo Sr., private, U.S. Army, 78th "Lightning Division," World War I. *Courtesy of Marie Cillo Pennimpede*

Jack Panella, Anthony Cillo, Pete Cillo, Liber Panella, Pietro Cillo, and George Jones (kneeling) get ready to leave for World War II, April 3, 1943. *Courtesy of Pete Cillo*

The Warriors

The borough has, in many ways, actively attempted to recognize those residents who served our country in conflicts from the Revolutionary War to today's conflicts. Knowing that it is not possible to accurately cite each who served, we offer a few representatives as a means of extending our gratitude to all.

June Atkinson-Day, World War II, U.S. Navy Reserve, specialist Q. *Courtesy of Jean Day*

Robert Terry Day, World War II, U.S. Navy, gunner's mate 2nd class. *Courtesy of Jean Day*

World War II—George Albert Gray, U.S. Army Air Corps fighter pilot with the 347th Fighter Group in the South Pacific. He flew 110 missions. *Courtesy of Gloria Gray*

The Wallet

In 1956 former Army PFC Pete Cillo received a letter from a priest in Sedan, Ardennes, France. In his letter, the priest tells how he found a wallet in a pew in his church with an attached note indicating the wallet had been found on a street in 1945. The note asked the priest to return the wallet to its rightful owner, but it didn't explain where the wallet had been from 1945 to 1956. In any case, the wallet was returned with ration and identity cards, photos, and 1,560 Belgian francs. Pete recalled being stationed in Belgium while attached to Gen. Patton's Third Army, and while riding in the back of a truck, the wallet fell unnoticed from his pocket.

WHO WAS THE FIRST MENDHAM WOMAN TO BECOME A U.S. MARINE?

ANSWER: MARGARET CATHERINE O'KEEFE

Chapter Seven: Protecting and Serving 143

Above: Iraq, U.S. Air Force—Master Sgt. Patrick M. Kelly was deployed in Iraq and Kuwait during the war in Iraq, and in December 1994 he served in Germany in support of the peacekeeping mission in Bosnia. *Courtesy of Patrick Kelly*

Above: World War II, U.S. Army—Timothy E. Pierson was attached to a motor pool in the Quartermaster Corps as a truck driver delivering supplies. *Courtesy of Tim Pierson*

Left: Vietnam Conflict, U.S. Army—Capt. Herbert W. Korte Jr., a pilot flying Huey transport and helicopter gunships for the 117th Assault Helicopter Company in 1967–68, flew more than nine hundred combat missions. Among other awards, he received the Distinguished Flying Cross, twenty-seven air medals, and the Vietnam Cross for Galantry. *Courtesy of Herb Korte*

Above: Korean Conflict, U.S. Air Force—Maj. Harry Sterner flew for the U.S. Air Force from 1954 to 1957 and later in the New Jersey Air National Guard from 1963 to 1976. His 108th Tactical Fighter Wing at McGuire Air Force Base received an Air Force Outstanding Unit Citation. *Courtesy of Harry Sterner*

Above: Joe Szoke at the Veteran's Memorial in the Borough Park. *Courtesy of Joe Szoke*

Left: Can you name this Navy lieutenant? *

Left: Kayla and A. Jonathan Loree, eleventh-generation Lorees, place flowers on the new memorial at the Hilltop gravesite of the Revolutionary War soldier Job Loree, who settled in Mendham in the 1740s. More than sixty Loree descendants gathered in the oldest section of Hilltop Cemetery as Job's crumbling headstone, placed in 1807, was rededicated and a new granite marker provided by the Veterans Administration was unveiled.

* Gerard Dolan

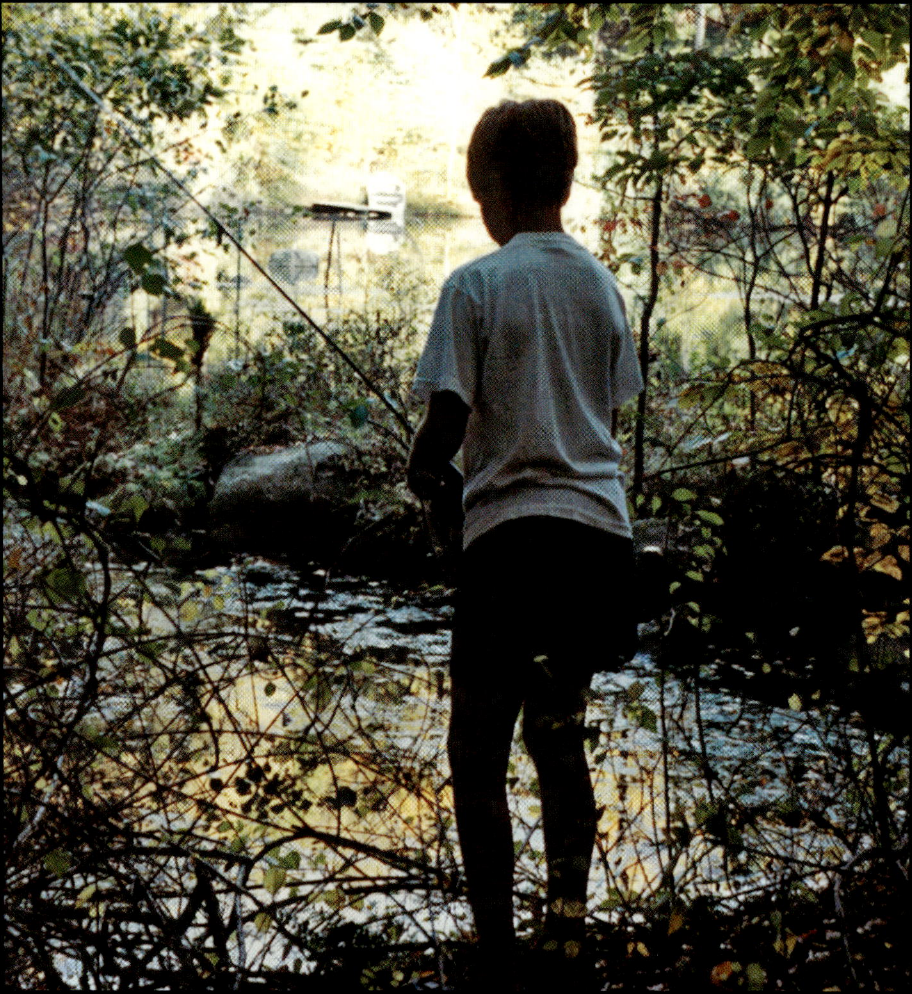

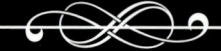

Chapter Eight
Outdoor Diversions

*The Lenape Indians would dribble a leather ball for miles—
this may make soccer the oldest sport in Mendham.*
—Charles Topping

Our Parks and Fields

Mendham Borough, a community heavily involved with sports, has been extraordinarily fortunate in its ability to provide facilities while minimizing the expenditure of tax dollars. In most instances, this experience has been a direct result of its residents' generosity.

The Borough Park

Located in the center of town, land for the Borough Park was purchased from the Babbitt sisters in 1923 for $3,500. The next year, Amzie Chambers offered to sell the borough a strip of land that would become Orchard Street, and he donated land that is now Park Street, thus creating most of the current park boundaries. By 1945 the park needed substantial renovation, and Cyril Birch has been credited for organizing the borough fire department as a source of labor to upgrade the facilities. According to Kate Emmons' research, Birch also donated the maple and fir trees that line the park, and for several years he had his employees maintain the land.

The Carriage House

Some seventy-five years later, the borough council approved funds for renovation of the ballfields and

Former Yankees batting coach Tony Ferrara instructs Mendham Little Leaguers. Coach Tony Grieco met him at a Yankees Fantasy Camp and invited Ferrara, who graciously came down from Cooperstown, New York, to instruct the Giants. *Courtesy of Bob Marino*

parking lot, but it rejected the plans for a building to house lavatories, storage areas, and even a snack bar as being too expensive. However, the cinder-block "shack" was crumbling down around the Little League volunteers and was in danger of being condemned.

As luck would have it, builder Pat O'Neill was working on a project off Prospect Street. Although he doesn't recall exactly who, when, or why the idea occurred—the moment of eureka—a notion developed that perhaps a historic 1800s carriage house doomed for destruction on the property right of way could be moved to the park. Developer Kevin Wilk, architect Nick Cusano, and Councilmen Larry Haverkost and John Andrus put their heads together, and it was deemed possible. With some architectural renovations included, Pat presented the borough with an unimaginable and unanticipated gift: if the borough would remove the old shack and prepare the foundation, he would absorb the expense of moving the structure to the ballpark.

It wasn't long before the carriage house, loaded on a huge trailer, was inching its way down Muirfield and Heather Hill, up Hilltop, and down Mountain to the park. Now resting securely between three baseball diamonds, "18 Prospect" serves as a shelter, storage facility, and meeting room for summer day camp and for all who use the fields.

Thoroughly unique in its design and shaded by trees planted in memory of Debby Gaffney and Peter Kenny, the structure both overshadows the more modern options and visually appears a perfect fit for its location.

Franklin Field

In the eighties, growing youth sports programs created the need for additional fields, which was brought to the attention of Councilman Lou Garubo. At a council meeting, DPW Superintendent Dave Crotsley suggested a piece of town property adjacent to the high school on Franklin Road, and Town Engineer Vic Woodhull agreed that bulldozing four feet of dirt from the west end eastward would create a flat playing surface. Although an economical way to develop a field, there were no budgeted funds.

After the council meeting, Garubo and Mayor Mike Ackerman adjourned to the Black Horse Pub to discuss a possible fundraising effort. As luck would have it, they bumped into Jim Gunther, who was asked if Gunther Motors might consider a donation. The answer was in the affirmative. Pub owner Anthony Knapp happened in shortly thereafter. Feeling they were on a roll, Garubo and Ackerman cornered Knapp, who also agreed to a donation, and Franklin Field became an overnight reality.

West Field

Finding the size of its membership making quantum leaps forward, the Mendham Soccer Club also found that adequate fields were rapidly

Top: 18A Prospect Street on location at the Borough Park. The trees to the right were planted in memory of Peter Kenny and Debby Gaffney. *Photo by Michael Gaffney*

Bottom: Gazebo with the War Memorial plaque in the foreground. A controversial project, the gazebo was to be built with donated funds and labor, but the council was eventually forced to contribute a substantial portion of the costs. *Photo by Michael Gaffney*

decreasing. They spotted a relatively promising area off West Main Street and approached the DeNeufville family, who owned substantial acreage in that area. With borough officials brought into the discussions, it was agreed that the family would donate enough land for a soccer field, and a right of way would be granted from Route 24 to the rest of the family-owned property.

One large field and a small practice area were designed, but some time later—additional fields still in demand—the town had a contractor working at the sewer plant, and part of the agreement called for the contractor to remove the extra fill by a specified date, a date that was not going to be met. Borough officials suggested a cure for the potential breach of contract: remove the fill at the contractor's convenience, but move it to the new West Field. The additional fill built up the far end sufficiently so that an additional full-size field could be placed at the site.

Left: The Mountain Valley Pool being built. In the foreground are Fred and Ruth Cramer, 1949. *Courtesy of Honey Belton*

Right: Enjoying Mountain Valley Pool when you could swim are (l-r) Ann Tiger, Charles Watkins, Theresa Parrillo, and Honey Parrillo Belton, 1950. *Courtesy of Honey Belton*

The Mountain Valley Pool, NOT the Mud Hole

Today's Mountain Valley Pond, the "mud hole," built mainly by citizen labor—from contractors to children—on land donated by Pietro Clementi, used to be a more popular center of activity than is currently the case. Even before the pond was built, you may have seen the Cillos shooing away cows from Clementi's nearby pond so they could swim, or maybe there was a baseball game to be played after cutting down the hay on what is now Florie Farm Road.

Much like the borough pool that did not get built in the 1970s, there were objections to the building of the "mud hole," with many deeming it too expensive. Only when in August 1948 Cora and Phil Parrillo, along with the Cramers, Halls, Moshers, and Cillos, organized a parade down Main Street in support of the pool did the tide turn. The parade, complete with cars, signs, and children on bikes, followed Mayor Bowers and Marshall Brill to the borough council meeting at Hilltop School. The group presented a petition to the council, which pledged $7,500 for construction.

Men came home after work to clear the land, and although the Belton boys plugged the drain and used the pond for a prededication swim, the facility opened for official swimming on Memorial Day 1949. Operating expenses were raised through a fund drive and a Coke machine located on site.

Once the "pool" was built there, it attracted passive recreation—two Jacks (Swatsworth and Turpin), years apart in their experiences, recall the area

Chapter Eight: Outdoor Diversions **149**

as a great place for a friendly stroll with whomever. There was more active recreation as well. As Michael Ackerman remembers:

"At the bottom of Mountain Avenue, where India Brook runs under the street and before the road begins its climb up the mountain, lies the Mendham Mud Hole. The dam, painted aqua at one point, held back the town's swimming pool—derisively called the Mendham Mud hole. This body of water served as the community pool and skating rink. Yes, Virginia, long ago, ponds froze solid for most of the winter, and the whole town could skate on the pond.

"The weekend after school got out marked the daily opening of the Mud Hole. Most everyone purchased pool tags and would swim there during the summer. The cars parked on the south side of the pond. (I remember there was an old chain link fence between the parking lot and the nearest home. The fence was overrun with Concord grapes, there for anyone to eat.) You were not allowed to walk along the water on the southern side, which was a shame because the southern side of the pond had the greatest concentration of frogs, snakes, fish and, of course, snapping turtles. You crossed over a bridge where India Brook ran into the Mudhole and were scrutinized by a guard sitting at a picnic table, looking for your pool tag. In truth, the guards didn't really care after the second week of the season, but if you were one of the guard's pets, you could be assigned this job, and you gave it all you had.

"Let me give you the lay of the land—or should I say water. After the sentry post, there was a sandy shore that ran into shallow water. It was here that the mothers set up chairs, talked, sunned, and looked after the smaller kids. A quarter of the way down the bank, the sand petered out, and there was a stretch of grass before the deep end. In front of the grass was the creamiest, most odoriferous black mud, perfect for a mud fight. In the deep end was a concrete dock, at the end of which was a diving board. It was here that as a child you aspired to play, but first you had to pass the seeming insurmountable Deep End Test.

"Swimming lessons were available from the guards and Mrs. Bergman—no first name ever existed for this woman, and even the moms referred to her as Mrs. Bergman. The mothers all wanted their kids taught by the inscrutable Mrs. Bergman. The air was filled with her never-ending 'Take a breath . . . blow,' you'll never make swim team until you 'take a breath . . . blow.' If you could then pass the Deep End Test—four lengths of the dock wasn't the tough part, the tough part was the entire town would watch—you were immediately drafted into the swim team. I wondered why a small child, who has swallowed a half-gallon of water passing the Deep End Test, would be such a find for the swim team. I later learned this was all part of the Mrs. Bergman/mom conspiracy. Swim team was every day from 8:30 a.m. to 11:30 a.m. The concept of daycare wasn't well developed in 1968. What better way to get rid of your kids for three hours when school was out. Moms who made use of this watery day care were the Driscolls, Donahues, McManuses, Healys, Hardimans (though Michael rarely got wet), Mahoneys, and the Enrights.

"The 'mud hole' got its name from the water color. It was always brown. Visibility was four to five inches. When you took your junior lifesaving test, they would throw a sand-filled Clorox bottle into the deep end, count to ten, and then tell you to find it. We lost dozens of Clorox bottles this way. The prevailing theory was that while you counted to ten, the bottles were swallowed by the creamy black mud. We always speculated as to what the guards would do if anyone really did drown and

Michael R. Ackerman. Courtesy of *Mike Ackerman*

go down. Guard names that I remember were Pat Courtet, Diane Miskel, and Barbara (who needs a last name when you were the least punishing swim teach coach). We rarely had male guards.

"One of the strangest things was that once a week, if you were one of the guard's pets, you could chlorinate the pool. To do this, you would punch holes in one of those five-gallon buckets of powdered chlorine, tie it to the back of an aqua aluminum rowboat (the dam, dock, slides, and even the boat were aqua as if maybe the water would take a hint) and row around for a couple of hours. This did nothing for inducing water clarity, and I doubt it did much to reduce the bacteria count in those millions of gallons of water, but it worked wonders at killing the sunfish that lived in the water. If you were one of the guard's pets, the next day you could row around with the five-gallon bucket and pick up the dead fish.

"Back to the swim team. As most people know, swimming is a race between contestants over a standard distance. The problem was there was no way to establish a standard distance in the "mud hole." You couldn't swim across the pond because that wasn't any of the standard 25-, 50-, 100-yard distances, and the snapping turtles owned the far bank. To solve this problem, the town sunk a number of poles into the mud 25 yards out and strung two-by-eight boards across the poles. To this were attached the lane ropes reaching out from the concrete dock.

"For 25-yard races, a couple of parents went out in a boat to determine the winner. If you had a 50-yard race and weren't good at a flip turn, you could just fake it a couple of feet early. This gained you a few feet on your opponent—no one was out there to check, and it wasn't like you were going to get a good push off the turn. Relay races were out of the question. Sometime in the early '70s, a full dock was built, and you couldn't cheat on your turns anymore because the parents were out there the whole time. My daughter, Jessica the swimmer, is fascinated as to how you knew to swim straight in your lane without a line on the bottom of the pool.

"Note, we were not the only mud hole. Our swim league was composed entirely of other teams that swam in ponds—except the wussies in Bernardsville, who had a concrete pool with lines on the bottom. Bernardsville was always skeeved out at away meets. (Does anyone remember how Horseshoe Lake had perfectly clear water, but the pond weeds grew all the way to the surface? If you drew an outside lane, your arm strokes pulled up the weeds.) Sometime around age twelve, only the hard-

Left: Hockey on the Mountain Valley Pool, 1990.

Right: You can fish not only in the pond but in the streams as well. If you're lucky, you get invited to the private "secret pond," which teems with bass.

Chapter Eight: Outdoor Diversions

Left: In addition to the pool, Patriot's Path has trails, barbecue pits, swings, and even water fountains to wash off the nasty bugs.

Right: The remains of the skating warming hut built by the Jaycees. Although open-sided, there was a wooden shingle roof that shortly became firewood (twice).

core stayed on the swim team. This was the age when as a boy, it was mandatory you wear one of those tight Speedo suits. It was also the beginning of the 'I won't ask, and don't you tell' policy. It went like this: you left the house at 8:00 a.m., met your buddies and didn't bother the same mother more than once a week for lunch. Then your mom, slyly, never asked if you went to swim team practice, and you threatened your younger siblings, 'Don't you tell Mom.' This always worked with my brothers, Tim and Jon, but Betsy, Susan, and Carole always told Mom.

"The swimming season wrapped up with the Labor Day festivities. Not everything was held at the borough fields. The day's events started at 8:30 at the mud hole. First was the potato hunt. The Jaycees would jam pennies, nickels, dimes, and quarters into potatoes. The potatoes were then thrown into the sandy, shallow end of the mud hole. Since potatoes sink and visibility was four to five inches, you felt around with your feet for the potatoes. I always thought it was strange that the Jaycees would do this because all those nickels and dimes were then squandered at the Pastime Club's booths at the borough field later in the day. After the potato hunt, there were the final swim races and even a diving contest. Then it was up to the borough fields for the bike and running races, ending with the fireworks. The next day school began, and the brown water of the mud hole was forgotten until December.

"This is written by one who does not fancy skating, and unless there are sticks and a puck, thinks the idea of skating rather pointless. At best, I believe skating is one of those Olympic sports that should not have a men's division. As I told Virginia earlier, lakes and ponds really did freeze solid in the past. I don't believe global warming is caused by humans, but I will agree that winters in the past were a lot colder. Our swimming hole in the summer became one of two town skating rinks. Two?, some of you may ask. Yes, some winters the fire company would plow the snow on the baseball fields into snow banks and then flood the ballfield.

"But the real action was down the bottom of Mountain Avenue at the very place we swam all summer. (I remember wondering why the water, which was brown in the summer, turned white when it froze. Even aqua would have made more sense.) Sometime in November, the families (most everyone had a family of at least five kids back then; the Courtneys and Wells had ten, while the Bowlands were the winners with twelve) would go to Archie's. Archie's was a kind of year-round flea market with endless outbuildings, located in Meyersville. In one of the outbuildings were hundreds and hundreds of worn-out skates that you could rent

Friends to the end, no matter which team they play for. *Courtesy of Jack Kuhn*

for the season for $1. Other than the families mentioned above, the whole family could be outfitted for a sawbuck. White figure skates for the girls and black for the boys—Archie's had no hockey skates.

"It was always strange that during the summer we were not allowed on the far bank or parking lot side of the mud hole, but when winter came, all the action took place on the parking lot side. There were rows and rows of Caprice Estate, County Squire, and Vista Cruiser station wagons—the SUVs and minivans of that time. There was a large rock on the southern bank. On weekends a fire was built alongside the rock. Nonskaters, pyromaniacs, and pregnant mothers (there was always a bunch of these) would gather at the rock while those who skated were out on the mud hole. If there was a hockey game, that took place on the northernmost side of the pond and was a place of fitful action. As was the case with most athletic activities of the day, it took a smattering of all ages between eight and thirteen to get a team together. The most exciting moment of skating was when a large groan ran the pond length, as the ice adjusted to the stress of those above. Everyone would stop for a moment, then activity would resume.

"Run-off from horse and cow farms upstream and changing expectations eventually made the mud hole impractical as a community swim hole. But when it did exist, it was as much a focal point of activity for Mendham residents as the borough fields are today."

Michael R. Ackerman, age forty-five, now lives in Malvern, Pennsylvania, and has a muddy pond behind the house that "I would never swim in and only freezes solid enough to skate on three or four days a year."

Sports, Sports, Sports

Call it obsession, call it passion—athletics in Mendham have drawn virtually the entire borough into a participatory mode. From the Pastime baseball and basketball teams of the 1930s to the highly competitive traveling teams of today, from four-year-old soccer players to sixty-five-year-old cricket players, the choices are endless. The following are just a few.

It's never too soon to start on the stick work. Cooper Lathrop suits up.

Chapter Eight: Outdoor Diversions

Baseball's Inventor

Strolling on Main Street after the Civil War, one might have passed General Abner Doubleday, who was reputed to be known as "marching," not walking down the street. While known as an officer during the Civil War, Abner Doubleday is best known as the inventor of baseball. He first came to Mendham as a guest at the Phoenix House and stayed, building his retirement home next to 13 Hilltop Road. He died in 1893, and the house was torn down in the 1930s. A memorial plaque to the inventor of baseball is located in the ballpark on Mountain Avenue.

Little League and Girls Softball

Mendham Little League was granted its first charter in 1977, and for much of its existence combined to play with teams from Chester. As the number of participants grew, the Mendhams formed an independent league, and borough and township players filled rosters without regard for their home address. Later, Harding joined the mix—but not to be mixed in with Mendham squads until All-Star play—and competition became intense.

During the late eighties and early nineties, the program began to offer greater opportunities for those Little Leaguers who wanted them. Competition in the Little League's national tournament on the road to Williamsport took place. For a time, Little League Inc. restricted outside tournament play, so decisions had to be made, and often Mendham All-Star teams would opt for playing up to twenty games in five weeks in various tournaments throughout the state.

The snack bar was going full swing three or four nights a week and Saturdays. The usual dogs and burgers were served, but a major draw was the homemade chili at Chez Jeff's (Dillon), and it was not uncommon to find a family-filled SUV with a less ambitious and perhaps less-discerning epicure/mom at the wheel arriving to pick up Friday night's dinner. As the coffers

Left: The Little League snack bar going full swing: Debbie Gaffney, Jeff Dillon, Penny Andrus, and Barbara Malloy serving.

Right: Pastime's Bob Collins and John Andrews present Tom Voynick the Babe Ruth championship plaque. *Courtesy of Bob Cleary*

The Ump

Each time a Little League coach finds himself alone, coffeeless, lining a field at 7 a.m. on a Saturday, he might think of the time and effort contributed by Brookside's Dave Hoadley. Retired in 2003 after thirty-five years, there may have been no volunteer with greater longevity than ex-marathon runner Hoadley, who umpired some seven hundred games from behind home plate at the Brookside Community Club. In an era when umpires, usually high school players, were paid, Dave not only never took a nickel, he would save the league money by eschewing the base umpire as unnecessary. And he never missed a call....

filled, better equipment was purchased, and to return something to the players, $10 would get parent and child a bus ride (with movie), hoagies, sodas, and a ticket to a Scranton–Wilkes Barre Red Barons AAA game. (One year's highlight was the rather rotund gentleman, two hot dogs, one in each hand, a super-sized beer lodged between his thighs, catching a foul ball as it submerged itself in the foam-filled Yeungling—and he barely spilled a drop.)

Although almost always facing teams from larger towns, the 1989 eleven-year-olds beat, among others, teams from Roxbury, Randolph, and Morristown to win the district championship. Greater success came when the nine/ten-year-olds won the 2002 district, then repeated in 2004 when the eleven/twelve-year-old club became district champs by being the first team in twenty-five years to win the double elimination tournament out of the loser's bracket. In doing so, they defeated Randolph East in two straight games to take the title.

The girls' softball program has joined with Mendham Little League, and Mendham won its first district title for the nine/ten-year-old division in 2000. They came back in 2001 to successfully defend.

The league has grown to more than 850 children, and some 350 parents volunteer as managers, coaches, team parents, commissioners, umpires, and committee members. A committee of twelve members now oversees almost seventy teams, including a fall ball program.

Mendham Babe Ruth

Mendham Babe Ruth, known as the Bi-County Babe Ruth League, began in 1964 when concerned fathers like Bill Bergman Sr., Jack Banks Sr., and Sam Tufts Sr. wanted their sons to continue playing baseball after Little League.

Teams of teenagers played the surrounding Somerset and Morris County towns, and state championship teams in 1977, '78 and '80 were coached by Bob Parish, Cal Hoffman and Mike Stewart Sr. The winning ways continued in both summer and fall ball leagues under Dom Paragano, Tim Miller, and, most recently, under Tom Voynick, whose team won a Babe Ruth State Championship in 2005.

The constant in the program, transcending the period from the mid-'70s to today, is Robert "Lou" Allain. More than winning state championships with assistants Art Bernstein and Bob Roselli in 1988, '94, and '96, Allain coached a brand of ball known to players and parents alike as "Lou Ball."

Mel Allen Puts Kid Team Over

Staff Correspondent.

MENDHAM—Small-fry baseball reaped a harvest in dollars and cents here last night when the New York Yankees' sportscaster, Mel Allen, voiced an appeal for funds at a game between the Mendham all-Stars and the Morristown Rotary team.

Allen, who came to the game directly after telecasting the Red Sox-Yankee contest at the Stadium gave a play-by-play description of the junior-sized action over a public address system. He spoke also over Radio Station WMTR at the conclusion of play.

Jack Dormer, president of the Mendham Midget League, said the organization, which was begun this year with four teams, had tough sledding financially. About 70 boys registered for the league, which was beyond expectations.

Comes Prosperity

Last night, Allen's appeal for funds, which was unprompted, changed the picture.

Six supporters of the league, all former local ball players, collected about $380 from among the 1,500 spectators and put the league back in the black.

Making it a perfect day, at least for the Mendham youngsters, was the fact the champions of the Morristown Little League went down 8 to 3 at the hands of their Mendham rivals. Johnny O'Brien was the winning pitcher.

How Mel Allen saved Mendham Little League—August 10, 1952. *Courtesy of Bob Cleary*

Chapter Eight: Outdoor Diversions

Left: Eleven-year-old New Jersey District 1 champs, 1989.

Right: Twelve-year-old New Jersey District Champs, 2004. *Courtesy of Jack Kuhn*

"LOUBALL"

To spectators, it appeared to be an environment where one knew that any opposing batter who swung and missed a curveball saw nothing but curves until he proved he could hit one; where the runners went from first to third on bunts down the third baseline; and where mistakes were tolerated but corrected.

To many players, "Louball" was more than just a game. Expecting a liturgy of tales about teenage baseball pranks, a former player, Jeff Andrus, was asked for his recollections:

"'Louball,'" as the practice of playing town-sponsored baseball for Lou Allain was affectionately termed, was the purest form of America's Favorite Pastime. As Ebby Calvin LaLoosh learned in Bull Durham: 'A good friend of mine used to say, this is a very simple game; you throw the ball, you catch the ball, you hit the ball. Sometimes you win, sometimes you lose, and sometimes it rains. Think about that for a while.' Such was the mantra heard by anyone within earshot of a Louball Game at Pastime Field on a Saturday afternoon in the summer.

"Allain had a knack for teaching the game by refusing to ignore its simplicities. As a third base coach, his signals for batters to bunt were two parallel fists clenched tightly in front of his torso. His signal for stealing to a runner was an index finger pointing to second base. A suicide squeeze was often initiated with an impromptu three-man conference on the third base line.

156 *Reflections on a Community:* Mendham Borough ∞ The Centennial 1906–2006

"Where other towns might have found it difficult to field a team each summer, Louball was anticipated by everyone who played the game locally. The prestige sometimes even eclipsed that of the high school or American Legion ball. And the lineup reflected that. Batsmen from towns that local players never heard of often defected from their own leagues—and would travel miles—for an opportunity to play Louball.

"Allain made the game fun, and he believed and invested in his players—often going to great lengths to get them recognized by college recruiters and scouts. But Louball lessons extended beyond he seventh inning, when after a game he would invite the squad back to his home, at the opposite end of Valley Way from Pastime Field, for a barbecue. He brought his players to Yankee games and followed them through their amateur careers. He was the consummate "baseball guy." He loved the game, and Louball taught its players to love it—and all that is synonymous with baseball—too.

"Just prior to a game scheduled a day after the death of a friend and classmate of the players, Lou sat the team down upon noticing that they were understandably numbed by the events of the day before. His message was simple, honest, extraordinarily profound, and I remember it like it was yesterday. It went something like this: 'We're about to play a baseball game. A game. What happened to your friend is life, but you're young. And because you're young, you don't know what I know,' Allain said. 'What I know is that there will be a lot more death in your life than you can now fathom, and a lot less baseball. Today, although it seems difficult, you can decide to go on with either one or both of them. I don't care which option you choose —if you want, we can all go back to our cars right now and go home —but my advice is that you choose both.'

"We played and won that day."

Jeff Andrus, thirty-two, now resides in Haddonfield, New Jersey, and was last seen building a backyard pitcher's mound for his eleven-month-old son.

Tennis

The Labor Day tournaments, a Mendham tradition that spans more than half a century and is fueled by the generosity of the Pastime Club and the dedication of enthusiasts like Carol Lindskog, DiDi Sharkey, Barbara McLoughlin, and many others, continues with thirteen tournaments attracting players of all ages.

In addition to the annual tournament, the dedicated efforts of these many volunteers have led to instruction for young and old alike, and in 1993, when Mendham joined forces with the United States Tennis Association to implement a USTA National Junior Tennis League, the program took a quantum leap forward. From fifty students in the first year to well over one hundred students in the ensuing years, play expanded beyond instructional needs to the development of a competitive program with local park and club programs.

None of this may have happened but for Mendham's "Mr. Tennis."

Top: Robert "Lou" Allain congratulates hurler Jeff Andrus after another Babe Ruth victory.

Bottom: Pregame parade for the old-time game commemorating the Abner Doubleday Field dedication: (l-r) John Wilson, Glen Coutts Sr., Gary Brady, Dan Donoghue, Jerry Jones, unknown, Glen Coutts Jr., Mike Stewart, Bruce Bergman.

Chapter Eight: Outdoor Diversions

Joe and Kathleen Huemer, grand marshals, 1985 Labor Day Parade.

Dedication of the Borough Courts to Joe Huemer: (l-r) Pastime's Dick Brede, David Huemer, Kathleen Huemer, and Mayor Chuck Reeves.

NJTL players and instructors, 1996: (l-r) Cameron Robinson, Alex Raddin, Tom Norton, Mike Bryce, Daniel Williams, Katie McLoughlin, Andy Raddin, Mark Williams, Dave Sharkey, John Sharkey, Graham Sharkey, Maureen McLoughlin. *Courtesy of DiDi Sharkey*

Joe Huemer

Many of Mendham's tennis-playing residents assumed that Joe and Kathleen Huemer bought their home on Park Street so that Joe would need only cross the street to play the game he loved so much. That assumption was incorrect; Joe and Kathleen moved to Mendham in 1948, but it took Joe some fourteen years to get the first court built at the Borough Park.

After graduating from Montclair State College and obtaining a master's degree at New York University, Joe spent World War II assigned as skipper of a minesweeper with tours in both the Atlantic and Pacific Oceans. Unable to pursue his favorite game during the war years, Joe returned as a teaching principal in Brookside and an avid tennis enthusiast in the borough.

He was a lead member of the committee of volunteers who raised the funds to build the first court at the Borough Park in 1962. Others included Dr. Clyde Bowers, Mary Lou Freeman, Anne Fulton, June Gunther, Marjorie Menagh Jenkins, William Murphy, Katherine Robinson, Penny Rutter, Eleanor Sturken, and David Tyson as well as wife, Kathleen. One fundraising event was the borough's first tennis tournament, which was, of necessity, held at a private court.

With the court finally built, for several decades Joe conducted free clinics for both children and adults. Recognized for his contributions to the community as a member of the Recreation Committee, director of many Labor Day tennis tournaments, a scoutmaster, a member of the Environmental Committee, and a diligent supporter of the development of the borough's portion of Patriot's Path, Joe was named as grand marshal of the Labor Day Parade in 1985. Joe's commitment to the town and its youth never waned, and he actively participated until his death in 1994.

Playing against Joe in the Labor Day tournaments always brought mixed feelings to his opponents—as badly as you might want to experience the joy of victory, it never felt right to defeat Joe Huemer—and many times, that was enough to provide Joe with the edge and the win.

Joe Huemer earned his nickname as Mendham's "Mister Tennis," and all those he touched were proud to see a plaque placed in his honor at the entrance to the borough courts.

LAX

Boys Youth Lacrosse began in Chester with the formation of a PAA club formed by former players Ron McGurn and George Rose. The early years saw steady growth as the community began to see what the coaches already knew: lacrosse is America's fastest sport on two feet, combining the speed, finesse, and individual play of hockey and basketball with the ruggedness of football. Literally hundreds of program "graduates" have played at Mendham

Top: Chester (Mendham) Lacrosse vs. Catonsville, Maryland, 1995.

Middle: Chester Mendham Boys, 2005.

Bottom: Girls' lacrosse. The feeder program has allowed Mendham High School to become a state lacrosse power.

Chapter Eight: Outdoor Diversions

Above: Shillelagh Shuffle prize winner Tommy Lauerman was awarded two TWA tickets to anywhere in the United States. He chose San Diego. *Courtesy of Dave Lauerman*

Top right: Mike Smith and his pipers lead the runners down the high school driveway to the start of the shuffle.

Bottom right: The start down East Main Street during a rainy early Shillelagh Shuffle.

High as well as local private schools, many reaching the highest levels in state play and going on to play in college.

Under the guidance of Halle Toia, girls' lacrosse began in the mid-nineties, and a program that had thirty participants in four grades in 1997 hit 120 in 2002 and is growing. Like the boys, teams play local towns, and the success of the program has been showcased at the high school level where the girls' team has competed for state championships, winning the title in 2005.

Running

I think we turn here—they can't expect us to run up that hill.
—Heard on a practice run for the Labor Day 10K

Despite its less than ideal, even daunting, topography, Mendham has been the site for a number of road races. The short-lived 15K (9.3 miles) proved to have too many hills to be enjoyable, and as a 10K (6.2 miles) from Mendham to Chester is almost entirely uphill, it, too, was doomed from the start.

In an effort to enhance the Labor Day festivities, the '70s saw the Mendham Area Jaycees sponsor a Labor Day 10K. The initial course finished with delightful trot up Corey and Cherry Lanes, around and down Prentice, and then a final sprint up the Talmage hill, past Hilltop Church to Hilltop School.

Walking over to watch the runners finish, Carol Heath chanced to meet one of her baby sitters, Debbie Enright. Always one to offer an encouraging word, Debbie's only comment was, "Don't worry, Carol, he's OK." Increasing her pace, Carol located one of Mendham's most competitive athletes, but not one of its best trained runners, husband Jerry, in the back of the borough ambulance. Mumbling something about it being a strategic error to attempt a sprint up the Talmage Hill, Jerry survived to run another day. But the course was altered the next year, and a more gentle finish was incorporated. However, due to a lack of manpower, the race vanished in just a few years.

"The Shillelagh Shuffle"

In 1980 two overweight, out-of-shape, ex-athletes, Ron Riescher and John Andrus, were attempting to repel middle age by training for and running in local road races from 5-mile runs to the NYC Marathon. Monday morning training runs were frequently spent recanting the inadequacies of the prior weekend race. At about the same time, Ron's son, Rob, reported that his St. Joe's class was searching for ideas for a fundraiser. With no experience and little forethought, a commitment was made.

A race was born with no name; it had no character until Debby Riescher brainstormed "Mendham 10K" into "Shillelagh Shuffle." Not perfect—not really appropriate for a race—it was a stroke of genius. The Irish theme, the Kelly green shirts with the dominant shamrock and shillelagh-toting elf set the stage. Entry lists were replete with Kellys, O'Briens, Murphys, and Dolans, and to two totally inexperienced race directors, it suddenly became a daunting challenge. Expecting perhaps a total of 150 runners for the Fun Run and 10K combined, a flurry of entries in the final week before the race pushed the number past 350. Most of the two nights before the race were spent furiously attempting to augment the shirt supply by hand-screening enough shamrocks to meet demand.

Much like the running community, the Mendham community bought into the idea. Fearful a proposed shutdown of Route 24 on a Sunday afternoon in March would be vetoed, Riescher and Andrus went to the borough police with hats in hand. Chief Cillo assigned Sgt. Dave Aussicker to the task, and the cooperation was outstanding. Aussicker not only enlisted help from the township police department, but he outlined a plan for volunteers to control traffic at some thirty intersections.

To ensure that everyone received the correct shirt, number, and handouts, a cadre of volunteers prepacked hundreds of envelopes, and between dusk and dawn, two-foot-long green footprints somehow appeared on the pavement along the race route. Volunteers from St. Joseph's—some seventy-five on race day—manned a variety of positions. The rain from the night before abated the morning of the first race, and with Peg Dick "commanding" a totally manual registration and Eileen Kelly handling the noncomputerized finish line, March 29, 1981, kicked off the first of more than a dozen Shuffles. Councilmen Barry Starke and Lou Garubo drove a pace car outfitted with colorful flags provided by John Wilson, and it was only fitting that local high school star Melissa Holm won the women's 10K. In year one, the race raised $1,500 for St Joseph's School. It was a truly "hometown"

Top: Shuffle race co-director Ron Riescher gets them lined up on Main Street. The race peaked at some one thousand runners.

Bottom: Sal Fondaco, Hal Korte, and Werner Engelmeier cool down after Mendham Patriot Run, 1981.

race, as parents ran with their children in the Fun Run and 10K, roller skating the course was allowed and, occasionally, an athletic canine was known to accompany his owner for the full 6.2 miles.

Through snow, rain, cold, and gloriously warm, sunny spring days, the Glucks, Bradleys, and Kellys, among dozens of other families, worked year after year as volunteers for more than a decade of races. Original sponsors Jimmy Mongey's Dublin Pub, Jerry Jones Mack, Lou Garubo's House of Charm, and Bill Dunn were loyal for the duration. The 369 runners in 1981 grew to 636 in 1983 (more than one hundred from Mendham), and in ten years the race grew to more than a thousand runners. Each successive year a shamrock was added to the shirt, and each year both the participants and amenities increased. Irish folksingers entertained before and after the run. In addition to the usual trophies, there were drawings for TVs, bicycles, and airline tickets, and the Lumbering Hulk Track Club offered trophies and prizes (mostly Guinness) to winners in the Heavyweight, Superheavyweight, and Cruiserweight divisions.

The single bagpiper in year one grew to an entire pipe band, which, under Riescher's guidance, led the runners down the high school driveway to the start on Route 24. As the runners looped up Cold Hill and down Mountainside, individual pipers were driven to key intersections along the hilly final few miles; and although the finish line at the Arboretum on Dean Road may have been beyond sight for the runners, the sound of the pipes would waft up to Sterling and energize those surging down the final three-quarter-mile stretch.

In its time, the Shuffle raised some $50,000 for St. Joseph's School, but the fundraising really became incidental to a community event that brought hundreds of neighbors together each year on a spring Sunday afternoon. (Riescher's postrace party wasn't bad, either.)

The Shillelagh Shuffle name lives in the form of a race in West Newton, Massachusetts—a 5K run sponsored by Paddy O's Pub.

Soccer

Today's West Morris Soccer club began as the Mendham Soccer Club in 1976 when there were enough players to form two teams and play against neighboring towns. Two former players and current coaches, Eric Steigerwalt and Bruce Schmeal, remember well their old coaches, Scottie King and Ron Barber, who were enthusiastic and opened the players' eyes to the world of soccer. One of the most

Top: A strong defense or "beehive" soccer?

Middle: Girls' soccer team picture—a very strong feeder program to the high school. 2005–6 Girls' traveling team—Sarah Hayes, Lea Senft, Megan Verde, Katelyn Gaffney, Claire Conklin, Paige Seavy, Julie Roettger, Christina Swift, Colleen Jennings, Arleen Delaney, Allie Long, Sarah Hogoboom, Kenzie Parker, Gabbi West. Coaches Bryan Seavey and Simon Moores. Missing: Emily Morrell and Coach Brian Gaffney. *Courtesy of Bryan Seavey*

Bottom: 1982 Labor Day—legions of soccer players march.

Top left: Twin Boro Bears running to daylight. *Courtesy of Kevin Kenny*

Top right: 2004 Twin Boro Bears Super Pee Wee Team, which went undefeated and untied. *Courtesy of Kevin Kenny*

Middle left: Bears cheerleaders, 1984.

Middle right: The 2004 version of the Bears cheerleaders. *Courtesy of Kevin Kenny*

Bottom: Steve Smith enjoying the game and a fine cigar.

vivid memories was that of the sideline coaching of Scottie, who would often yell in somewhat less than dulcet, but delightful, Scottish brogue, "What kind of a pansy move was that?"

Now merged with Chester, the club boasts an incredible 1400 players with one hundred intramural and twenty-three travel teams—and as has always been the case, hundreds of volunteer parents in support.

Twin Boro Bears

Mendham has combined with Chester to form the Twin Boro Bears, and judging by the consistent success of Mendham High's football program, the Bears are doing something right.

Chapter Eight: Outdoor Diversions 163

Pat Dannenbaum and Rob Mortensen on a Recreation-sponsored ski trip.

Day Camp talent show, 1989.

2003 Holly Trail Sing-Along at the gazebo.

Left: Day Camp entertainment.

Summer Day Camp

Summer Day Camp has been a popular activity for Mendham children for many years. Under the tutelage of Dave Garrison, now-retired Mountain View physical education teacher/coach and borough recreation director, the camp was often oversubscribed. It not only provides recreation for hundreds of children, but it also provides summer jobs for many of our teenagers.

The camp as we know it was not Mendham's first. A newspaper article written by Beatrice Douglas years earlier tells about the summer jobs of Mendham's teenagers between their junior and senior years. "One of the most interesting projects engaged in by two young girls was the play school conducted by Barbara Ayers (Haslam) and Mary Ann Enright (Stauffer). The barn on Barbara's family property on New Street was the site for the school. Barbara and Mary Ann remember walking to the children's houses to pick up and deliver their charges. The fourteen youngsters enjoyed a daily schedule that included the flag salute, two songs, mid-morning snack, story time, and a daily arts and crafts project—not a whole lot different from today's camp.

Above left: Nancy Barnes Morales, former Mendham Day Camp director and current physical education teacher.

Above right: Mary E. Stauffer and Barbara Ayers Haslam may well have had the borough's first summer day camp in the '50s. The girls took care of fourteen young charges who enjoyed a daily schedule of games, snacks, arts and crafts.

Chapter Eight: Outdoor Diversions

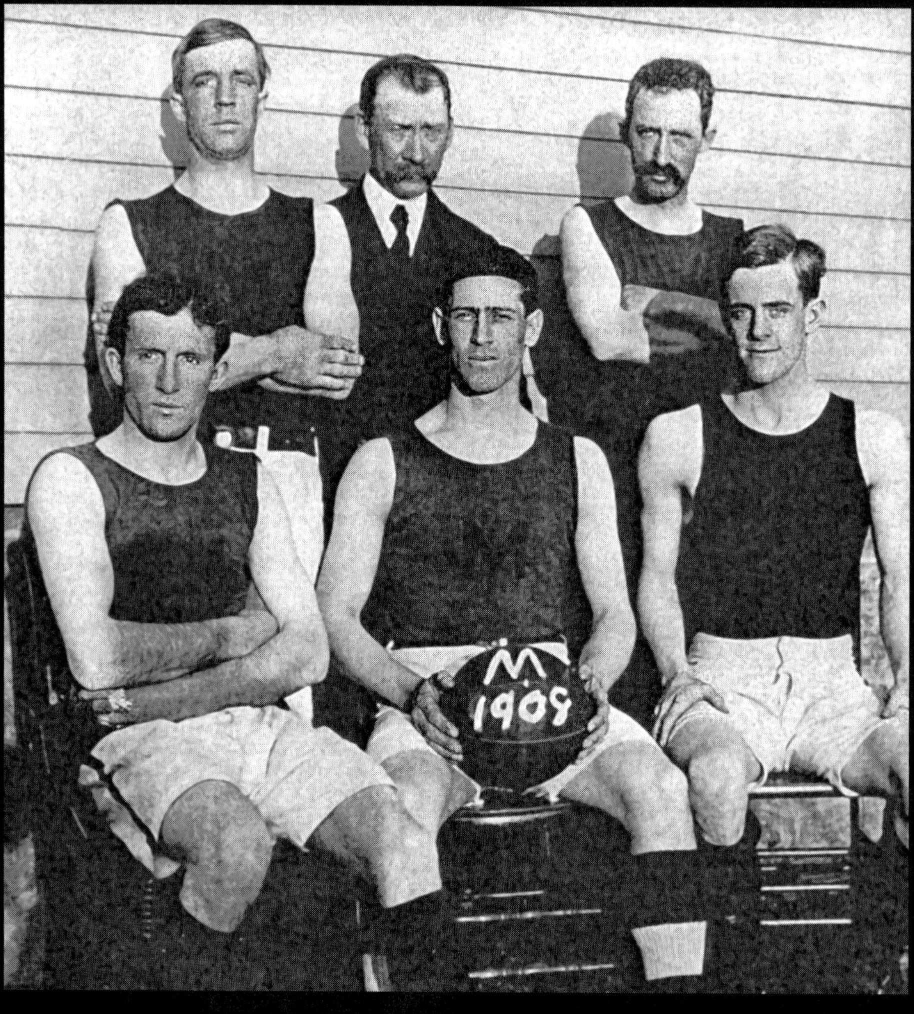
M
1909

Chapter Nine
Community through Common Interests

It is not so much our friends' help that helps us as the confident knowledge that they will help us.
—Epicurus

The Farmers and Sportsman Game Association

Possibly Mendham's first "club," local hunters organized the Farmers and Sportsman Game Association as early as April 21, 1898, at the request of property owners in the western Mendham Borough and Mendham Township area who sought protection from predators for their cattle and property. Today, the stated objective of the organization is to better protect fish and wild game and to aid in carrying out the laws of the State of New Jersey for the same and also to assist in the propagation and protection of fish, wild game, and the sports of hunting and fishing. Another goal is to advance the social interest among its members. The association has some fears as to its future—in 1960 there were fifty-five hundred acres of land to hunt, but due to the encroachment of housing, there remains only twelve hundred acres.

Mendham Garden Club

Mendham Garden Club held its first meeting at the home of Ella Mockridge, founder and first president, on July 6, 1932. Members were to be solicited from each of Mendham's churches and from the "mountain people" (Chester ?), and by the second

Scouting has a long history in the borough. Here, Den 17 exhibits their usual exuberance. *Photo by Ginnie Beutnagel*

Top left: This cabin on the Thomas Property serves as an entry point to land that the Thomases allow the Sportsman Game Association to use.

Top right: Award-winning Phoenix House garden, 2006. The Garden Club is currently planning extensive renovations for the garden.

Bottom: Annual Garden Club Plant Sale, held in the shopping center.

meeting, there were twenty-six members. The club decided that there should be no dues. Programs were to be provided each month by a member whose birthday occurred that month, and often the program was simply to visit the member's garden and to, peculiarly, play cards. Although by 1934 dues were set at twenty-five cents per meeting attended, then doubled in 1938 to fifty cents, it was clear additional funds were needed, and the first annual plant sale, which continues today, was held in 1934. The profit was $5.55.

After the Phoenix House was donated to the borough in 1937, the club received permission to embark upon a major project by creating a Phoenix House Garden, and by 1939 Mayor William Cordingley and landscape architect Martha Brookes Hutchinson designed the garden, and work had begun. A second large undertaking began in 1942 when the area at the Oak Tree Triangle (Cold Hill and Route 24) was cleared and planted. Both areas were greatly improved in 1969, and recognition came to the club in the form of three prestigious awards from the Sears Foundation for local beautification projects—the Triangle, Phoenix House, and Garabrant Center. Another award from the Sears Roebuck Foundation was received in 1971.

The Garden Club's many current projects include donations of shrubs and bulbs to the children's garden at Hilltop School (in memory of Dr. F.

Clyde Bowers), flowers for the Lyons Veterans Hospital, Greystone Hospital, and for roadside beautification. In addition, the club has been instrumental in donating trees and bushes to the Mountain View School and elsewhere for planting on Arbor Day.

When in 1966 there were proposals to use the Great Swamp as a site for a new major airport, the Garden Club became very active in its opposition by supporting the natural preservation of the site. The borough library has been a Garden Club benefactor, receiving many book donations from club members. Earl Barnes designed the original bookplate for donated volumes, which are often made in memory of deceased husbands.

Left: First exhibit of Mendham Garden Club dish gardens by charter members. *Mendham Borough archives*

Right: In this May 8, 1969, *Observer Tribune* photo, a Sears representative presents three awards to the Mendham Women's Club for its community beautification projects. *Courtesy of Observer Tribune*

Junior Women's Club

Founded in 1957, the Mendham Junior Women's Club is a service organization formed by and for the young women of the Mendham Area who have sponsored charitable, educational, and civic activities in the surrounding communities for almost fifty years. The mission of the club is to unite women of the Mendhams and neighboring communities to volunteer their time, talent, and energy in creating an organization that sponsors various projects to support a broad spectrum of needs within the borough.

Among the many projects organized by the club's Health Committee are an annual blood drive held in partnership with the American Red Cross, the St. Patrick's Day luncheon for the Mendham Area Seniors, and adult and child CPR training. Winter Marketplace is an annual event to raise money for a scholarship for a local high school senior, and club members make crafts for the schoolchildren to buy for siblings, parents and teachers.

The Home Life Committee's goal is to enhance family life by holding traditional events such as the Labor Day Games and Races, a Bunny Brunch, and a visit from Santa. Recent fundraisers have included a Ladies Luncheon, Casino Night, a Dinner Dance, and a Fashion Show. Monies raised at these events go to various charitable organizations in the area.

Promoting high standards of education within the community and enhancing public awareness of community needs are the assignment of the Public Affairs and Education Committee, and annual events include the Thanksgiving Food Drive, a spelling bee, and the selection of scholarship recipients.

Chapter Nine: Community through Common Interests

Top left: Junior Women's Club members Mrs. Hamilton and Mrs. Steigerwalt help with the dog clinic in 1967. The dogs were tattooed with their owners' Social Security number and added to a national dog registry. *Courtesy of Mrs. R. Steigerwalt*

Top right: Junior Women's Club members serve at the annual St. Patrick's Day luncheon for the seniors, 1993. *Courtesy of Junior Women's Club*

Bottom: The Junior Women's Club contributed funds and was a driving force behind the Borough Park playground, shown here during construction. *Courtesy of Junior Women's Club*

In addition, there is an Environmental Committee charged with heightening public awareness and respect for our environment. To achieve this goal, the committee members plant bulbs for seniors, participate in local Earth Day activities, and plant trees in the community. In the event there are local families in need, a committee is devoted to assessing the needs in any given situation, reporting back to the membership, and leading efforts to take appropriate action. Approximately fifty-five regular members participate, and their contribution to the community clearly exceeds their numbers.

Mendham Area Jaycees

During the expansion era of the 1960s, the proliferation of new housing drew an influx of many young men and women who were looking for ways to become involved in their new community. An outlet for these energies became available when a group of young men sought and were successful in obtaining approval to sponsor a Mendham Area Jaycee chapter. In 1964 Richard McCabe became the first president of the combined borough and township chapter.

As the Jaycees grew, they threw themselves into a variety of community, social, and athletic projects. Perhaps the two most significant goals of the group involved the community's young children and the environment. Jaycees chapters nationwide sponsored annual Pass, Punt, and Kick competitions for boys and girls from ages six to fourteen. The Mendham Jaycees held the competition at the Borough Park and were pleased by the amount of local participation and proud to cheer on those who made the finals at Giant Stadium. On Labor Day they assisted in various contests, races, and games, and for a number of years they served as marshals for the parade. Jaycees earned funds to contribute to charity by selling tickets for working at the Jaycee Classic football game between the Giants and a team from Philadelphia. Funds went to projects such as purchasing a picnic table and grills for India Brook Park, and they purchased the first electronic scoreboard for Mendham High's football field. A major effort was put into constructing (twice) a warming shelter for ice skaters at the mud hole. Unfortunately, vandals destroyed both the original effort (they used the wooden roof shingles for firewood) and the second attempt.

Unlike today, no organized recycling program existed in the borough, but a solution was found in a partnership between the Jaycees and Mendham Borough. A recycling center was established on the grounds of the Public Works Department, and with the assistance of Superintendent Dave Crotsley, bins for glass, cans, and paper were established. On weekends the Jaycees staffed the center.

This task was considerably less arduous than the famous firewood fundraising project where the chapter sold firewood to local residents at reduced prices. No doubt an idea hatched late in the evening on meeting night, the Jaycees didn't just buy in bulk and resell at a marginal mark-up; instead, they obtained approval to cut down and cut up dead wood from the town parks, split it without the use of a mechanical splitter, then loaded, unloaded, and delivered it by the armful.

It was no wonder they felt they deserved both recreational pursuits and after-hour playtime, and for years major attractions to joining were the boisterous casino night, oldies dances, Labor Day Float parties, and family picnics held by the chapter. Fun flashed from Old Mill Park in Ralston to Deerfield in the borough to Brockden in Brookside; participation was enthusiastic, and legends were born. The Jaycee athletic endeavors lacked success in the early

Left: Peter Kenny chopping Jaycees firewood. It is said the wood chopping made the local paper and was key to getting Pete elected to the town council. *Courtesy of John Wilson*

Right: Bob Greenberg watches Tom Ferrara at a Jaycees night out. *Courtesy of John Wilson*

days, but in the seventies the ranks grew, phone calls were made, and the Jaycees became a dominant force in the local men's softball leagues as well as in the statewide basketball and touch football Jaycee tournaments. Fielding a group of aging "exhausted roosters" supplemented by the youthful Patrick "Packy" O'Brien, the Mendham Area Jaycees did on occasion capture the New Jersey state football title, defeating teams with players some ten to fifteen years their juniors.

But as the community aged and the reservoir of young males under forty began to dry up, the decision was made to dissolve the Mendham Chapter.

Mendham Seniors

In the late 1960s, a few friends in the Mendham community met regularly for a small social get-together. Whether simply having lunch, playing cards, or taking an occasional trip, they found that they enjoyed spending their retirement together, and as time passed, the group grew, and help was needed to plan and manage the various events. With the assistance of Julie Peters and Sandra Swanger, a more structured organization was provided. In October 1969, the friends decided to formally organize as a Senior Citizens Club. By January 1974 the membership grew to thirty-eight, then fifty-two just one month later, and by June the membership had climbed to seventy people. By the end of 1974, there were more than one hundred members.

Initially, the meetings were held in various members' homes, but as the club grew, meetings moved to the Phoenix House, Pastime Club, and then finally to the Garabrant Youth Center on Wilson Street. But the Garabrandt Center needed repairs and had no heat, so winter meetings moved to the various local churches until the Garabrant building could be rebuilt into a year-round facility. In 1978 the Youth Association offered the building to the borough. It was accepted with open arms, and a new gathering place for the seniors was established

By 1980 the borough had obtained a federal grant of $80,000, and, with an additional $14,000 for the driveway, was able to make extensive repairs. Additional funds were obtained through contributions of private citizens, businesses, banks, clubs, and professionals.

The dedication of a refurbished center took place in June 1982. A founding member of the seniors, Mrs. Francis Garabrant, was in attendance, and she fondly recalled the era when the site of the center, owned by husband Vernon's family, was a farm housing fifteen hundred laying hens. At the time, Wilson Street was a mere cow path.

In 1992 additional improvements were made—the interior was painted, a thick layer of insulation was installed above the drop ceiling, keeping enough heat in the building for comfort, and the members all waited for the

Top: Mendham and Madison Jaycees get together ca. 1973. Jaycees include (l-r) Paul Lyle, John Patera, and Ron Riescher. Also, Tom Lamb (sixth from right), Bob Wollinger (fourth from right), and John Wilson (third from right). In front is Adam Riescher. *Courtesy of John Wilson*

Bottom: The beginning of Jaycees athletic success began around 1973. The Jaycees played in the town league as "House of Charm" (see hats) and as "Jerry Jones Mack." Back row (l-r): George Travis, John Wilson, Lou Garubo, Jerry Jones, John Carolin; front row: John Andrus, Dick Whiting, Ron Hazelton, Jim Calloway, Dan Bayha.

At the Hershey Farm buffet: Dot Keupferle, Ann Fondaco, and Marie Pennimpede. *Courtesy of Vi Lioudis*

Seniors on stage during the Mount Snow, Vermont, trip in 2004: (l-r) Ann Mills, Alex Barth, and Viola Lioudis. *Courtesy of Vi Lioudis*

Members at the Garabrant House for the hat competition—Marge Myer, Carol Tomicitch, and Mickey Fagan. In rear, Shirley and Bill Grier. *Courtesy of Vi Lioudis*

day when they could call the Garabrant Center home. A gift of a piano was available, and the borough staff was able to transport it to the seniors. A Christmas party was planned, and the seniors were able to plan and participate in many programs, as well as from eight to ten trips per year. There were lunches and musical programs at Mountain View School and Mendham High; trips to Vermont, the Paper Mill Playhouse, the Garden State Art Center, and Allaire State Park, as well as participation with floats in the Labor Day parade.

As in the beginning, the club follows the same procedure they follow today—a flag salute, silent prayer, and the singing of national songs. Officers are elected annually, and volunteers head various committees, including the all-important joke committee. The seniors find additional support from the schools, as the seniors have been tutored on the use of their computers; Junior Women's sponsors luncheons, and they have been invited to lunch and entertainment at Holly Manor. Half the invited speakers are informative in content, while the rest are pure entertainment.

The seniors remain a well informed, lively, interesting group whose ages range from fifty-five to one hundred years of age. Total membership is 107, and when the club celebrated its thirty-fifth anniversary on October 25, 2004, members Madeleine Post, one hundred years of age, Daniel Davidson, ninety-eight, and Ruby Krupp, ninety-seven, attended. As much as the members appreciate all those who come before them, the citizens of the borough certainly reciprocate with their thanks to the contributions made by today's seniors.

—From secretary's minutes of Ann Wilkens printed in the book *20 Years of the Mendham Seniors, 1969 to 1989*, and Viola Lioudis, former secretary and program chairperson

Roxiticus Golf Club

South of Bernardsville Road, Walter P. Bliss, a wealthy investment banker, purchased two Ballantine Farms and built Wendover, a magnificent estate complete with ballroom, horse-training track, sculptured columns, and marble fireplaces. In addition to the expansive downstairs entertainment areas and many bedrooms, hidden back staircases would take one to the upper floor where seemingly dozens of small bedrooms were necessary to house the hired help.

Mr. Bliss died at the age of fifty-three, and his widow would remain at the estate until her death in 1962. The property reputedly was offered

Top: The seniors group at Mount Snow during the 2004 trip. *Courtesy of Vi Lioudis*

Middle: Seniors on the Thousand Island Trip: (l-r) entertainer, Marion Petersen, Enid Somer, Viola Lioudis, Ginni Grassi, and Lou Shioleno. *Courtesy of Vi Lioudis*

Bottom: Golf goes on at Roxiticus Golf Club despite the wreckage of a light aircraft after an emergency landing. *Courtesy of Roxiticus Golf Club*

The Minstrel Shows

During the 1930s, the famous minstrel shows were held at Hilltop School as fundraisers for both individuals and organizations. Although he never performed himself, John Enright put the shows together and directed them. For years, props and costumes were stored in the Enright home. Anyone who wanted to be a part of the shows was allowed to participate, and the sell-out performances were eagerly anticipated by all. Local newspapers ran articles announcing out-of-town guest stars, but the shows were clearly a town event. As Kate Emmons remembers, "We had so much fun. I always participated in the shows through helping with the scenery and props, selling tickets, or singing in the chorus. They were great times." They were typical minstrel shows of the era—songs, dances, slapstick humor, and corny jokes aimed at local politicians and prominent citizens.

for sale to the Kellogg Company for the construction of a research center, but ultimately the mansion on "Millionaire's Mountain" captured the attention of a group of golf enthusiasts and investors.

Jerry Volpe, the owner of the Englewood Golf Club, was to construct the course on land that Bern Shanley would purchase and lease to the club. Their intent was to open an exclusive men's club that would become the Augusta National of the North. Thanks to a suggestion from one of the founders' wives, the club was given the name Roxiticus Golf Club, and by 1966 the course was completed and the club incorporated.

Unknown to many, the club's activities included fishing, and for a period of about five years, golf bags not only contained persimmon woods and irons, but also one's favorite fly rod. Fishing at one of the club's ponds was a fairly common occurrence; after all, there was little delay in the round—the ponds were stocked. By 1973 the club transitioned from being an exclusive men's golf club to a family club and added facilities including both a swimming pool and tennis courts.

A devastating fire in late 1979 destroyed the beautiful old mansion and took the lives of the club's manager and his wife. Despite the lack of insurance funds, the membership was determined to replace the building, and within one year, the clubhouse was constructed, and Roxiticus again became one of the finest clubs in the area.

Mendham Borough Historical Society

In 1996, to prepare for the borough's one hundredth anniversary milestone and to give a voice to the historical character of the community, Mayor Charles Reeves asked Sally Foy to mentor the establishment of a historical society. A meeting to organize the society was held at the Phoenix House on

PROGRAMME

Opening Chorus	Entire Ensemble
"When My Dream Boat Comes Home"	Jerry Panella
"Copper Colored Gal"	Gerry Pulcanella
"One, Two, Button Your Shoe"	Charles Moeri
"Pennies from Heaven"	Joseph Dormer
"The Martins and the Coys"	Ken Garabrant, Jr., Bill Shanks, Victor Gilsdorf, Jim Lounsbury, Franklin Becker
"Serenade in the Night"	Charles Day
"With Plenty of Money and You"	Tobe Guerin
"In the Chapel in the Moonlight"	Walter Mosher, Vincent Parrillo, Jimmy Pierson, Peter Cillo
"Did You Mean It?"	Ethel Kagan, Joseph Emmons, Jr.
"There's Something in the Air"	Jerry Emmons
Banjo and Guitar Duet	Donald Morton, Bill Snyder
"Down Among the Sugar Cane"	George Hankinson
Jimmy Downey's Dancing Tappers	Helen Reed, Edith Lobel, Bernice Callahan, Isabelle Rosoff, Lois Callahan, Irene Holbig
"Did Your Mother Come from Ireland?"	William Fagan
"Trust In Me"	Catherine Emmons
"Little Old Lady"	Francis Pierson
"Hey, Babe"	Jimmy Sullivan
"Gee, But You're Swell"	Gertrude Lade
Jersey Woodchoppers of Pottersville	Jim Baker, Charles Ammerman; John, Kenneth and Russell Lindabury
"You Do the Darndest Things, Baby"	Freddie Martin
"Goodnight, My Love"	John Parrillo
"What Will I Tell My Heart"	Rose Colantuono
"Alexander's Ragtime Band"	Doc DeGroodt
Closing Chorus	Entire Ensemble

FINIS

The 1937 Mendham Minstrel Show program. The show was held at Hilltop School for the benefit of St. Joseph's Parish.

Chapter Nine: Community through Common Interests

June 25, 1996. Founding members included Mayor Reeves, Mrs. Foy, Charles Topping, Sandra Larsen, and Kathleen Marino. Mrs. Foy was named chairperson and, later, president, a position she held for the next five years.

The focus of the society is to bring together those individuals or groups interested in the history of Mendham Borough. Specifically, the society discovers and collects material that helps to establish or illustrate the history of the area, along with objects illustrative of past and present life, conditions, events, and activities of the borough. In cooperation with borough officials and the Mendham Free Public Library, the society provides for the preservation and accessibility of historical materials.

The society has taken great pride in the leadership role it assumed to organize the archives of the Borough Library, and credit goes to Marie Pfeifer for having diligently filed and cataloged thousands of documents and artifacts previously scattered in basement piles. New in 2005 was a genealogy contingent introduced by Peggy Oswald, who manages a nearly complete computer database of Mendham family histories. This activity spawned the active participation of the society in the rededication by the Loree family of the gravestone in Hilltop Cemetery of Revolutionary warrior Job Loree.

Past president Henry Roe introduced the program to present awards to individuals and organizations whose contributions demonstrate outstanding achievements in historic preservation. Henry organized the society's most successful fundraiser, a tour of the James Cole House on East Main Street. Current President Bob Jephson mentors the society's Labor Day Parade float, which recently received an award for its representation of the one-room school. Kate Emmons, borough historian, was honored as 1996 parade grand marshal, and the society served as grand marshal in 2000.

The 1997 House Tour of selected homes in the historic district served as a forerunner of many subsequent tours. Annually in September, the third grade classes at Hilltop School are given a tour, and using a guide written by Sandra Larsen and Ruth Smith, docents such as Mike Ackerman, Bob Jephson, Don and Newly Preziosi, and Charles Topping point to the significant architectural features and styles representative of Mendham's rich legacy and to the contributions of Aaron Hudson and other early builders.

On May 15, 2005, the society hosted an open house at the Phoenix House to showcase the old former roadhouse's restoration. Home for the society is the Phoenix House, where the group displays historical artifacts restored professionally, with services donated by Richard A. Moormann. Included are an eighteenth-century Federalist-style mirror and a second mirror once belonging to Elizabeth Phoenix. A Gould grandfather clock, restored by Dr. David Sperling, stands in the second-floor conference room.

Top: Mendham Borough Historical Society members Charlie Topping, Henry Oswald, and Peg Oswald during the Centennial Celebration. *Photo by Diana Callahan*

Bottom: Showing off the historical society's model of the Phoenix House during the Centennial Celebration at the Borough Park, Misters Jephson, Grievo, and Smith. *Photo by Diana Callahan*

Mendham's Newcomers and Neighbors Club welcomes new residents with a series of programs that include book discussions, bowling, bridge, gourmet dinners, mah-jongg, walking groups, wine- and beer-tasting parties, and playgroups. *Courtesy of Ginnie Beutnagel*

Newcomers & Neighbors Club of the Mendhams

Welcomes you to meet your neighbors and make new friends

*Become a member
Get involved
Have fun!*

For more club information please visit our website at: www.new2mendham.com

Mendham Brownie Troop 839. Front row: Mia Farlekas, Ally Marino, Kendrick Forbes-Doust, and Isabelle Rullo. Middle row: Meghan Cichocki, Maddie Egerter, Kaitlyn Walsh, and Kara Klemme. Back row: Gabby Cano, Sara Trank, Samantha Marucci, Noelle Kervick, and Samantha Apgar. *Photo by Bob Marino*

Mendham Newcomers and Neighbors annual clown party at the Garabrant Center with Sprinkles the Clown. *Photo by Eileen Lupo*

The Misery Club

In a world of highly organized groups, the epitome of a small-town club may well have been the unchartered, ruleless "Misery Club." This nontraditional group began in the 1950s as an invitation to visit and chat. Misses Anderson, Colwell, Banks, Fagan, Blaine, Hobie, and Watson were members of a group whose goal was, according to a December 12, 1955, Daily Record newspaper article, to "shake the blues away." Mickey Fagan recalls that it began as nothing more than friends deciding it was best to be with friends. Instead of meeting and chatting on the street, the group met at one or another's home to drink coffee, to finish their sewing, and to talk. It was a concept that brought friends together for more than thirty years.

The Pastime Club

Present and future Pastimers have a right and unusual heritage which they should cherish and selfishly protect.

—F. Clyde Bowers
Chairman of the Board of Trustees 1939–60

At various times, day and night, one might notice men of various ages entering a white clapboard building, the Pastime Club, in the midst of our historic district on Hilltop Road. Most have seen members sporting Pastime Club jackets and hats selling Labor Day 50/50 raffle tickets in front of King's on summer weekends. If you have children, you likely have been to a birthday celebration at "the best little bowling alley in America." Many of us know these few simple facts about the club, but until now we didn't know its full story.

The Pastime Club, one of Mendham's oldest groups, is a unique men's club with a rich history of community service. The club's current motto—Progress in Sports—hardly does it justice in reflecting the extent of its contribution to the community. Even the founding members' expressed purpose of "promoting and encouraging athletic achievement" barely hints at the club's impact. The preamble, read at each monthly meeting by the president, speaks of enhancing the interest and welfare of our community, and there can be no question about the effort of the 260 members to achieve that goal.

The Pastime Club façade on Hilltop Road. Sign points to the bowling lanes located behind the club. *Courtesy of Bob Cleary*

Dr. F. Clyde Bowers said, "Present and future Pastimers have a right and unusual heritage which they should cherish and selfishly protect. Once lost, it can never be reclaimed." One might debate what that heritage is, but there can be no argument about how the impressive results were achieved—volunteerism, hard work, cooperation, and community spirit are all words that come to mind, and any outsider (because few of us are not touched by

Top: Although the motto changed to Progress in Sports, this group of Pastime Softballers seem to ascribe to the original Pastime Is a Good Time. Back row: Walt Rockafeller, Bill Menagh, unknown, Alfred Gilliam, Greenlaw, Cyril Birch, Jack Dormer, John Parrillo, Joe Fondaco, Ken Steffen. Front row: Philip Parrillo, Frank Martino, Bob Oweiler, Jerry Parrillo, Fred Crammer, Gunnar Johnson, Dr. Bowers, Lou Mercurio. *Courtesy of Honey Belton*

Bottom: The Tin Can Sailors march in the 2005 Labor Day Parade. *Courtesy of Leo Baehler*

the club, few are really outsiders) can see this common thread woven through its history.

The club's start was somewhat rocky. It was founded at Leo Woodhull's house on June 24, 1915. Walter Rae was elected president, Walter Gunther was vice president, and George Woodhull became secretary. The initiation fee was 50 cents; monthly dues were 10 cents. Additional members were recruited, and subsequent meetings were held at the Black Horse Inn. The first motto was: Pastime Is a Good Time. According to Dr. Bower's history, the goal was simply to create a fraternal society that would promote sports—from quoits to baseball. Given the nominal amount for dues, it is not surprising the club failed—twice. The third time was a charm, and the club's resurrection occurred in 1938.

Walter Le Monnier served as president of the reorganized venture, and the club returned to sponsoring basketball and baseball teams as well as pinochle and quoits tournaments. Almost immediately, it reached out to the community by sponsoring a Christmas party for local children as early as December 1938. Fundraising was accomplished through various raffles.

As the club grew, it began to search for a permanent home, and in 1941 it purchased the current building located at 3 Hilltop Road for $2,000. Not a bad deal, but there was only a grand in the treasury, and the building was so dilapidated that the local banks refused to grant the club a mortgage. Eventually, however, the mortgage was obtained privately, and work began. Per Dr. Bowers, "No time was lost in renovating our new home, all of which was done by volunteer labor. All club members, skilled and unskilled, participated.... Every night, Saturdays, Sundays and Holidays, someone could be found removing plaster, shelves, porches, etc." By December 1941, meetings were held in the new facility, but with the outbreak of World War II, some 50 percent of the club membership answered the call. During the war years, building material was scarce, so basements, barns, and attics were scoured for sinks, stoves, furniture, and fixtures needed to complete the job. Efforts were made to accelerate the work so as those who served returned, they would have a place to meet.

By 1947, the club's facilities began to be used by various community groups. Building uses ran the gamut from dancing school to polling place. Outdoors, club-sponsored baseball and basketball teams continued their winning ways. Labor Day celebrations, started by the club in 1943 and, later, in 1951 and held in conjunction with the Borough Recreation Committee, consisted of races and games held at both the Borough Park and the Mountain Valley Pool. Much of the three days of activity converged at the Mountain Valley Pool. Older members may recall that the carnival had fewer rides and booths, but had a large dance floor where, for 10 or 20 cents a dance, you could dance to Tigger and the Lady Bugs, an all-girl band.

Top left: A pre-Pastime 1909 basketball team. Supporting these teams was one reason the club evolved.

Top right: Pastime ball team about 1940. Back row: Lawrence Lowery, Jack O'Keefe, Bob Bockoven, Bob Sullivan, Joe Viola. Front row: Lloyd Belton, Liber Panella, Donald Quimby, Pete Cillo, Joe Grassi, and Alan Banks. Kneeling: Calvin Hoffman. *Courtesy of Pete Cillo*

Bottom: Another generation of ball players around 1950. On ground: Jimmy Crammer, Slug O'Brien. Seated: Fred Crammer, Jack Dormer, Benny Ginter, John Parrillo, Roger Belton, David O'Keefe, Junior Cacchio, unknown, Billy Menagh. Second row: O'Connor, Ralph D'Agastino, Bill O'Donnell, Gusie Day, and Murph Rae. *Courtesy of Honey Belton*

Legend of the Beer Cans

When Pastime Lanes was under construction, "foreman" John Parrillo would station himself in the center of Mendham each evening to assemble a work crew from among the men returning home from their jobs. Did he entice them with some liquid refreshment? We don't know the answer to that question, but in 1997, when the old wooden lanes were removed to make way for the synthetic ones, workers found evidence that the "myth" is most likely true. They uncovered some rusted beer cans inscribed with the names Roger Tirrell and Jim Panella from underneath the alleys, where the two faithful club members had placed them for posterity.

With its finances on firm footing, the club expanded its activities, and with the large interest in bowling, a committee was formed to study the possibility of finding a place for the alleys. When the committee members stumbled upon the availability of four used alleys in Dover, they acted quickly, purchasing them with their own funds. Dr. Bowers refers to the group as the "scheming committee," who "wanted immediate purchase, not thinking where we might construct a building for the alleys."

The answer was to purchase from the borough a small piece of land behind the Phoenix House, expand the club, and, again, with volunteer labor, build a home for the four lanes. Every member of the club contributed to the building effort, and on October 29, 1953, George S. Thompson rolled out the first ball. Automatic pin setters would come later, but the alleys were opened to league bowling, and leagues were established—men, women, high school students, and children participated.

Later, the club would open the lanes to the public on Sunday afternoons for open bowling, and the memory of enjoying the intimacy and relaxed atmosphere of bowling with the family in a four-lane facility remains for those who had the opportunity to partake. In addition to serving as a home to numerous leagues, the lanes remain available to host innumerable bowling parties for participants of all ages.

In 2005, due to new fire code regulations, the club was told it could no longer cook under a tent at the annual Labor Day celebration. In the old tradition of Dr. Bowers, and emulating earlier Pastimers, the membership embraced the new challenge and solved the problem. Knowing full well the club would later need a better alternative, a core group of members collected donated materials and built a make-shift cooking shelter. Later, a permanent solution was brainstormed.

While in the process of awarding the contract for the Labor Day rides, the officers and trustees negotiated with the new vendor, as a signing bonus, a used French-fry trailer. During winter 2006, the same group of skilled and highly motivated members slowly stripped the old trailer and began to

Shooting a rack at the club are (l-r) Doc Bowers, Herschell Lyons, John Parrillo, Jack Pugsley, and Bert Grey ca. 1950. Courtesy of Bob Cleary

Wall of Honor

During a renovation of the clubhouse basement in January 1998, a panel was removed from a built-in bookcase, revealing twenty photographs of Pastime Club members in uniform. Also found was a plaque dedicating the Trustees Room to Robert A. Ferguson, the first resident and member of the club to lose his life in the fight for freedom during World War II. A Navy submariner, Ferguson died during the battle of the Solomon Islands in September 1942. Later in 1998, a few dedicated members and veterans decided to create a place of honor for these photos. The Trustees' Room initially was considered, but it was determined the members on the "Wall of Honor" would get the attention they deserved in the upstairs game room, where they would be seen more frequently by members and guests. Most of the photos were moisture-damaged, but a club member with the appropriate expertise stepped forward and was able to restore them. Pictures of newer members have been added over the years, and these include men who served in all branches of the military and in conflicts that include both world wars, Korean Conflict, Vietnam, the Cold War, and the War on Terror.

The Pastime Club Wall of Honor commemorates those members who served our country. *Courtesy of Bob Cleary*

renovate it by installing the club's cooking grills. Pressure was intense. The club had promised the Borough Recreation Committee they would cook all the hot dogs and hamburgers for the Centennial Celebration. Once again, dedication to the community prevailed as club volunteers came out in force, and on May 20, 2006, the renovated food trailer grilled truckloads of hamburgers and hot dogs and served soda and ice cream sandwiches to the community. Despite the intense heat in the trailer, the members knew their new food wagon would work. Cutting a new window in the trailer eliminated the heat problem, and the grills were now ready for the onslaught of Labor Day customers.

Pastime Club members volunteered not only to help their community, but they have volunteered to fight for their nation as well.

Currently, the club serves as host to Tin Can Sailors (Navy veterans), who have marched in the Labor Day parade since 1993. When inclement weather caused problems for the sailors' Labor Day picnic, the club opened its doors to the veterans, and since 1995, it has hosted the postparade reception. The club proudly honors these heroes each Labor Day.

The club's main fundraiser is the long-standing Labor Day carnival featuring games, refreshments, and the fireworks show on Monday night. Over the last few years, the club and its members have helped fund a tournament-quality girls softball field in Mendham Township and a lacrosse equipment shed; has provided new plaques for winners of the club's annual athletic award at Mendham High School; donated to the Morris County Challenger League Program for special-needs kids, and has provided funds for the

For the Record

Each year more than three thousand young men and women in the Mendhams and Chesters participate in school- and community-based athletic teams and other programs supported by the Pastime Club. They include:

Mendham Babe Ruth Baseball   Mendham Labor Day Tennis Tournament   Mendham Fall Baseball
West Morris Soccer Club   Chester PAA Basketball   Mendham Swim Team
Mendham Chester Girls Lacrosse   Twin Boro Bears Football   Mendham Cross Country
Twin Boro Bears Wrestling   Mendham Magic Track and Field   Pastime Lanes Youth Bowling
Mendham Ice Hockey   Special Olympics of New Jersey   Mendham Little League
Chester Mendham American Legion Baseball   Mendham Chester Patriots Youth Wrestling
Mendham High School Competition Cheerleading   Mendham Borough Flag Fund
West Morris Mendham High School Project Graduation
Mendham Borough Police Fishing Tournament   Mendham High School Veterans Memorial
Mendham Fire Department One Hundredth Anniversary

American flags flown on Main Street in the borough after September 11, 2001. Just recently, the club supported the new Veterans Memorial at Mendham High School. The Pastime Club Field (at the end of Valley Way) was named for the Pastime Club A's, a baseball team in the Morris Majors. In 1982, the club was a major contributor to the initial manual scoreboard, flagpole, and dugouts at Pastime Field. In keeping with the tradition and its dedication to athletics and the community, in 2005 a new remote-controlled scoreboard was funded by the club as well as privately by some of its members.

The club not only continues to reach out to the community, but it also reaches out to its members as well. The welfare committee supports those in need by sending cards to members and their families who are hospitalized, and through e-mail signage at the club, other members are alerted so they can lend aid. There is a call list for anyone who may need a ride to the doctor or the store, and when one of the members passes away, flowers are sent and donations are made in his name.

To the community, the Pastime Club has clearly become more than the sum of it members. In large part, funds raised by the group support youth athletics by providing donations to a large number of programs. Some forty-five hundred area children participate in and experience the benefits from these programs. Although these numbers were likely never imagined by Dr. Bowers, perhaps they do represent the heritage and tradition he encourages the membership to cherish and protect.

Larry Paragano and Steve Peck flipping burgers in the renovated trailer. *Courtesy of Bob Cleary*

Chapter Nine: Community through Common Interests   183

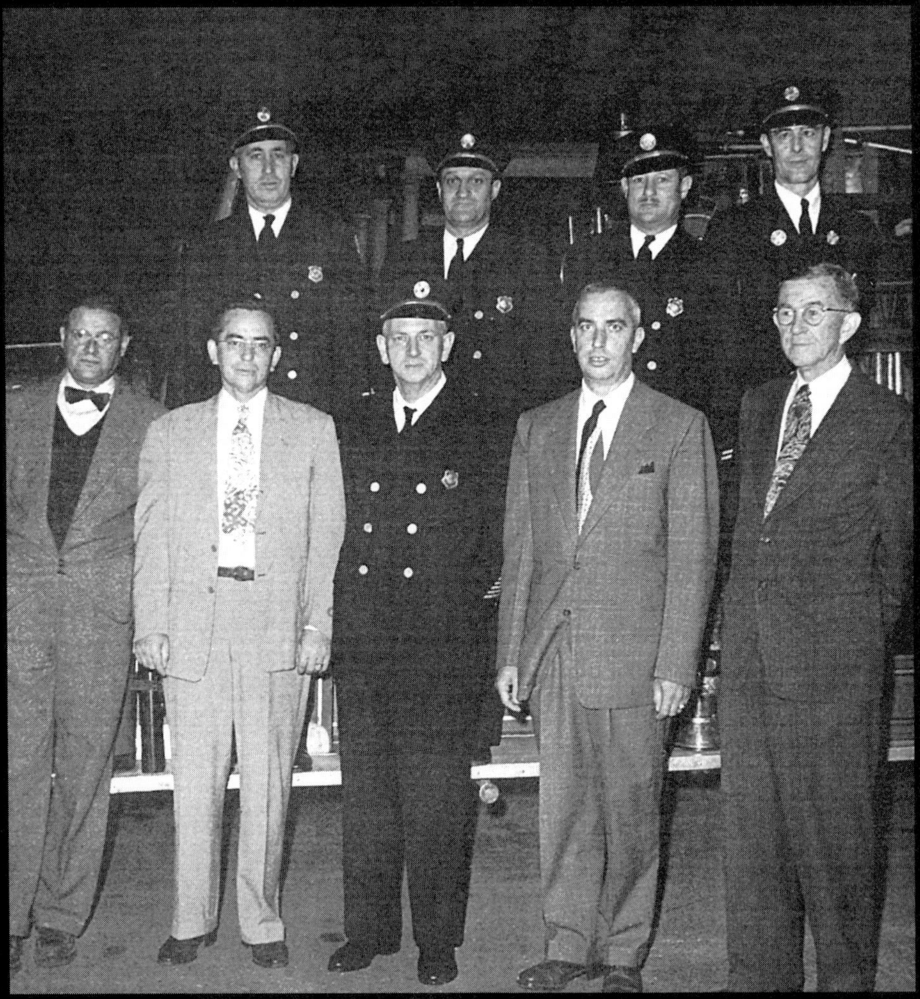

Chapter Ten

By the People, of the People, for the People

We hang petty thieves and appoint the great ones to public office.
—Aesop

It was June 21, 1981, and my daughter's wedding was scheduled for 4 o'clock at Hilltop Presbyterian Church. Our house was a flurry of activity of caterers, flowers, girls getting dressed, and the clock ticking. The groom was at the church pacing while groomsmen cracked jokes. Imagine our panic when our minister, Rev. Bob Phillips, asked for the marriage license.

License? License? said the groom. "No license, no marriage," was Rev. Phillips' response. This was quickly followed by a soon-to-be-mother-in-law, who made a call to Borough Clerk Marie Pfeifer's home. Marie made a quick trip to the Municipal Office and arrived at the church, with license, in time for the "I do." Where else but in a small town?

—From an article by Rickie Kelly, "Mendham Moves," www.mendhammoves.com

The first borough council meeting was held on June 18, 1906, and the governing body of six councilmen and a mayor took their oaths of office. Our form of government has not changed.

What has changed is the number of volunteer boards and committees upon which the borough now relies. Without these volunteers contributing to the oversight of our town, it is difficult to imagine

The fire department honors Robert O. Snedaker's contributions to the borough with a memorial plaque. "Sned" passed away in May 2004. Tom Berenbak helps Mrs. Snedaker attach the plaque. *Courtesy of Mendham Fire Department*

185

life in the borough as it is now enjoyed. Appointees to no less than a dozen various boards are voted on each January 1, and the thousands of hours spent by them can never be properly recognized.

Volunteer service by borough residents is vital to our quality of life.

Mayors

E. W. Elliott	1906–1917
Dean Sage	1917–1922
Charles H. Day	1923–1934
William Cordingley	1934–1936
Michael Coghlan	1937–1938
Frank Freeman	1939–1940
William Cordingley	1941–1942
James L. Bruff	1943–1946
F. Clyde Bowers	1947–1952
L. M. Thompson	1953–1956
Walter Rockafeller	1957–1960
John W. Dippel	1961–1964
Andrew Fletcher	1965–1970
Robert E. Mulcahy III	1971–4/1974
Harold A. Ketchum	5/1974–1978
Michael A. Ackerman	1979–1990
C. William Steelman	1991–1994
Charles S. Reeves	1995–8/1997
Michael A. Ackerman	8/1997–1998
Richard G. Kraft	1999–2006

Councilmembers

G. S. De Groot, M.D.	1906–1921
William N. Phoenix	1906–1913
George Delp	1906–1913
J. K. Burd	1906–1913
J. M. Hoffman	1906–1913
E. L. Garabrant	1906–1930
Dean Sage	1914–1917
J. Smith Gunther	1914–1934
Charles H. Day	1917–1922
Frank Woodruff	1922
Frederick R. Guerin	1922–1930
George S. Sutton	1923–1930
William DeVore	1927–1938
Clarence McMurtry	1927–1936
Michael Coghlin	1930–1936
Edward Talmage	1931–1934
Hugh M. Babbitt	1931–1939
Frank Freeman	1931–1938
Richard Farrelly	1935–1939
Dore Apgar	1937
Benjamin Mosser	1937–1946
Walter Gunther	1938–1942
Ferdinand Jelke	1938–1942
James L. Bruff	1939–1942
Thomas A. Carton	1940–1946
Frank Prior	1940
Francis Prior	1941–1942
Willard Carley	1943–1946
William Coghlan	1943–1946
Walter Rockafeller	1943–1946
Henry Landon	1943–1946
Cyril H. Birch	1947–1950
David F. O'Keefe	1947–1950
Edward Barnes	1951–1952
Raymond Greenlaw	1951
John W. Stutesman	1951
Robert M. Thomas Jr.	1951–1956
John W. Dippel	1953–1960
Harold W. Traudt	1952–1964
Henry Gette	1953–1956
William VonMeister	1952–1955
Howard Dean	1957–1970
Andrew W. Fletcher	1955–1964
John Parrillo	1957–1960
Francis Hewens	1961–1964
Phillip Parrillo	1961–1971
John Dormer	1965–1973
Robert Muir Jr.	1964–1970
Robert E. Mulcahy III	1965–1970
Vernon Garabrant	1965–1970
Philip R. Arvidson	1971–1975
Harold Ketchum	1971–1974
C. William Steelman	1971–1975
Ralph Williams	1971
Michael Ackerman	1972–1978
Peter Martin	1972–1977
Frank Peters	1974–1985
Kent Christiansen	1975–1976
Ruth Smith	1976–1987, 1992–1994
Michael Stewart	1976–1985
Stewart Cowell	1977–1980
Paul Kelly	1978–1980
Barry Starke	1979–1987
Peter Kenny	1981–1992, 1996
Cortez Ritchie	1981–1986
Richard Kraft	1986–1994
John Manley	1986–1988
Gerard Dolan	1987–2004
Louis Garubo	1988–2006
Charles Reeves	1988–1994
Robert Snedaker	1989–1991
James Cillo	1993–1995
John Andrus	1995–2004
Robert Marino	1995–2000
Theodore Mazzacapo	1995–1996
Lawrence Haverkost	1997–2005
John Smith	1997–2000
Neil Henry	2001–2006
Stanley Witczak	2001–2006
Dave Murphy	2005–2006
Barbara Stanton	2005–2006
Brad Badal	2006

Borough administrator Ralph Blakeslee stands under the portrait of Robert Snedaker.

Mayor E. W. Elliott—the borough's first. *Mendham Borough archives*

MENDHAM'S AMERICAN FLAGS WERE ORDERED FLOWN AT HALF-MAST STARTING JUNE 11, 1979. WHY?

ANSWER: ON THAT DATE, MOVIE STAR JOHN WAYNE DIED. MAYOR ACKERMAN, A HUGE FAN, ORDERED THE FLAGS FLOWN AT HALF-MAST.

Fire department picture from the late 1950s. (Many department members also served as elected officials.) Back row: Philip Parrillo Sr., councilman; Howard Dean, councilman; Jacob Lewis, Dick Clark; Front row: Gunnar Johnson, Dr. F. Clyde Bowers, mayor; Walter Rockafeller, mayor and councilman; Raymond Greenlaw, councilman; and Bill Coghlan, councilman. *Courtesy of Honey Belton*

Councilman and Mrs. Peter Kenny and Mayor and Mrs. Charles Reeves at Councilman Garubo's wedding, 1994.

Above: Board of Adjustment members Steve Peralta and Charlie Schumacher. *Photo by John Andrus*

Left: Lesly Henry, Councilman Dave Murphy, and Planning Board Chairperson Alexa Lewandowski enjoy a laugh at the centennial. *Photo by Diana Callahan*

Mayor-Elect Neil Henry gets some advice from ex-mayor Michael Ackerman. Among a lengthy list of town services, Mike served as mayor for fourteen years and as councilman for seven years.

Tax collector Rosalie Lauerman and Helen Cleary at the centennial. *Photo by Diana Callahan*

Above: Mayor Steelman hands out the Steelman Award to Jamie Eilbacher and Jeff Day.

Left: 1982 staff at the Phoenix House—Rosemarie Quilty, Sue Giordano, Marie Pfeifer, and Hannah Eaton.

Sue Giordano, borough CFO; Doug Wright, Sewer Department superintendent; Tom Miller, DPW superintendent; and Maureen Massey, town clerk, at the centennial. *Photo by Diana Callahan*

Above: Placing a memorial at the East Main Street, Tempe Wick Road Triangle in 1981: back row, council members Cortez Ritchie, Frank Peters, Peter Kenny, and Mike Stewart; kneeling, Ann Moore and Mayor Michael Ackerman. *Courtesy of Mike Ackerman*

Left: Longtime Planning Board member Penny Kopcsik responds to "thanks from the borough residents" during the parade.

190

Four of the borough's longest-serving elected officials: Lou Garubo, nineteen years; Dick Kraft, seventeen years; Ruth Smith, fifteen years; and Gerry Dolan, eighteen years. *Photo by John Andrus*

Above: Land use coordinator Diana Callahan.

Left: Waiting for the start of the Labor Day 2005 parade: (l-r) Stan Witczak, Neil Henry, Gerry Dolan, Lucy Monahan, Larry Haverkost, Dave Murphy, Barbara Stanton, and Lou Garubo. *Photo by Diana Callahan*

Bibliography

Observer-Tribune article, "Phoenix Family Memories," October 17, 1968.

Emmons, Catherine M. *Through the Years in Mendham Borough*, 1973.

Foster, Janet W. *Legacy Through the Lens, A Study of Mendham Architecture*. Scott Printing Corporation. Copyright by the Mendham Free Public Library, 1986.

Hall, Ted. "The Great but Very, Very Late Bank Robbery." *Life Magazine*. January 5, 1962.

"Jersey Lightning in Mendham," Fall Walking Tour, October 5, 1997. Mendham Borough Historical Society.

Mendham Centennial Articles, *Observer-Tribune*. May 14, 1981.

Mendham Fire Department 1905–2005, "One Hundredth Anniversary."

Mendham First Aid Squad. "Fiftieth Anniversary, 1940–1990."

"Mendham Historic District," Mendham Borough Submission to the National Register of Historic Places, submitted May 1999.

Mockridge, Ella. *Our Mendham,* copyright by Sarah T. Lamken, 1961.

Mueller Map, Mendham Borough—1910.

Rae, John W., *Images of America, The Mendhams.* Charleston, South Carolina, Arcadia Publishing, 1998.

Sanborn Map—Mendham Borough , 1923.

Swiencki, Judy. "Pastime Lanes, The First 50 Years." October, 2003.

The Mendhams. Mayor's Tercentenary Committee, copyright 1964 by the Mendham Township Committee, Brookside, New Jersey.

Turpin, John K., and Thomson, W. Barry. *The Somerset Hills,* Vol. 1. Far Hills, New Jersey: Mountain Colony Press, 2004.

Turpin, John K., and Thomson, W. Barry. *The Somerset Hills,* Vol. 2. Far Hills, New Jersey: Mountain Colony Press, 2005.

Wright, Helen M. The First Presbyterian Congregation, Mendham, New Jersey. Jersey City, New Jersey: Helen M. Wright, "Camp News," 1939.

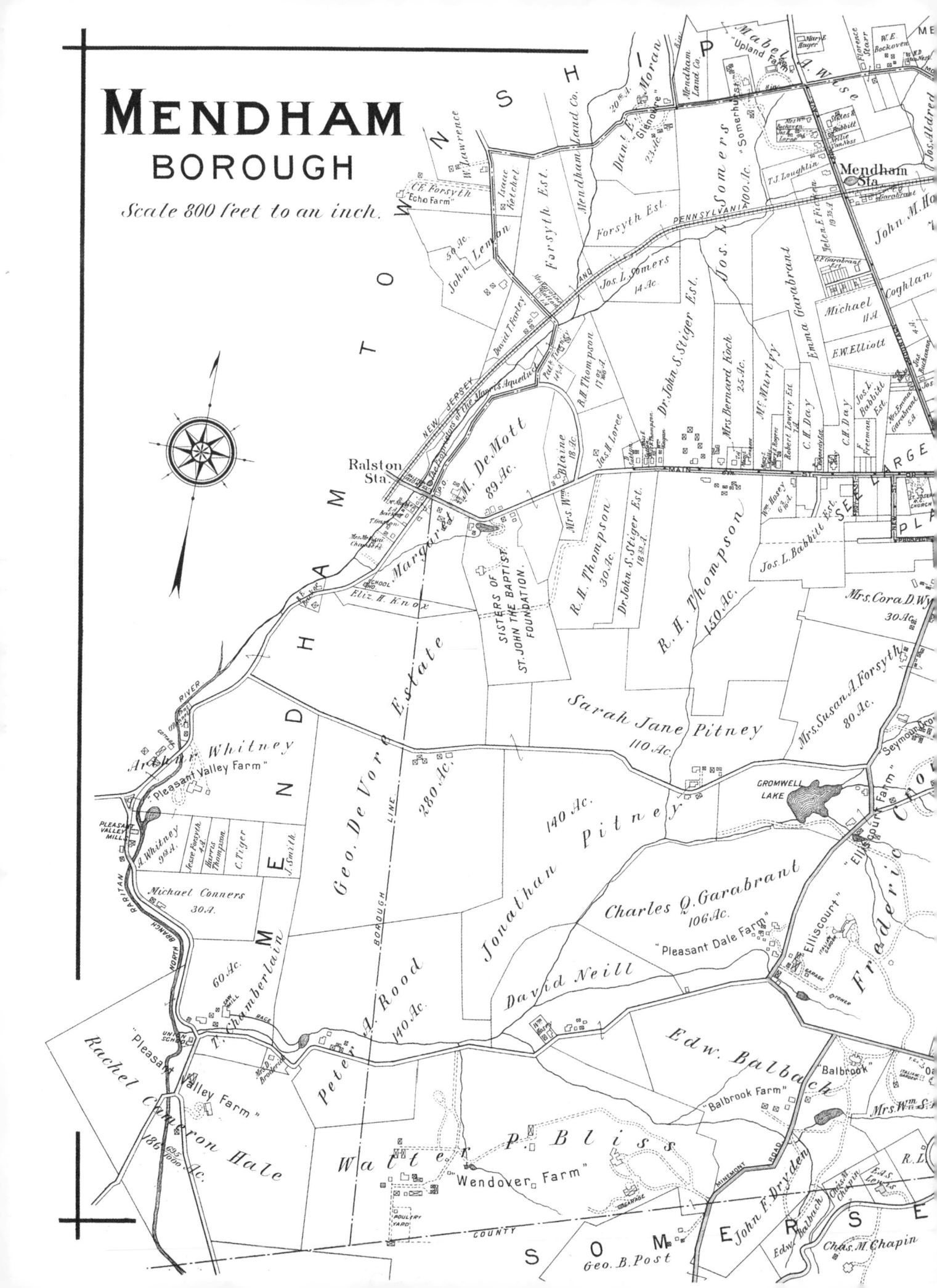

MENDHAM BOROUGH

Scale 800 feet to an inch.